VISIONARY ENTREPRENEURSHIP

Building a Future through
Purposeful Innovation.

VISHAL VINDA
VIJAY PALYEKAR

LIGHTHOUSE PUBLISHING SOLUTIONS

"DEDICATED TO THE MEMORY OF A BELOVED SISTER:
REMEMBERING VIPALI VINDA VIJAY PALYEKAR"

*Dedicating a book to someone is a significant gesture that shows
how much they have influenced your life and inspired your work.
This book is dedicated to my beloved sister, Late Vipali Vijay
Palyekar, who left us all too soon. Vipali was not only my sister
but also my confidant, my mentor, and my biggest supporter.
Growing up, Vipali and I were very close. She was always there
for me, offering encouragement and guidance when I needed
it most. She was the one who introduced me to the world of
entrepreneurship and inspired me to pursue my dreams of
building a successful business. I remember sitting with her for
hours, discussing different business ideas and how we could make
them work. She believed in my vision and was always there to
offer a helping hand whenever I needed it.*

*When I decided to pursue acting, she supported me
wholeheartedly. She was always the first one to watch me act,
offer feedback, and cheer me on. Even when I faced rejection and
disappointment, she encouraged me to keep going and reminded
me that failure is just a stepping stone towards success.*

*Later, when I started my own LIC agency, she was again my
biggest supporter. She helped me navigate the challenges of
starting a business, offered valuable insights, and even connected
me with potential clients. Her unwavering support gave me the
confidence to take risks and pursue my dreams.*

*Unfortunately, Vipali passed away before she could see the full
extent of my success. But her spirit lives on in everything I do. Her
love, support, and guidance continue to inspire me, and I know
she is watching over me, cheering me on from wherever she is.*

*This book is a tribute to her memory and the impact she had
on my life. I hope that it inspires others to pursue their dreams,
just as she inspired me. It is a reminder that even in the face of
adversity, we can find strength and motivation in the people who
love and support us.*

*To my dear sister Vipali, I dedicate this book to you with all my
heart. Thank you for everything you did for me, and for being the
best sister anyone could ask for. I hope that wherever you are,
you are proud of what I have achieved and continue to achieve in
my life. I miss you dearly, but your memory will live on forever.*

CONTENTS

PREFACE

Entrepreneurship has always been a vital force in shaping the world's economy and society. From the iconic entrepreneurs of the past who revolutionized industries to the contemporary leaders who are creating innovative solutions to global challenges, I have always been inspired by the impact of entrepreneurs on our world. However, as we enter an era of unprecedented technological advancement and social and environmental upheaval, I believe it is becoming increasingly essential for entrepreneurs to focus not just on their own financial success, but also on the impact of their business on the world.

This book, "Visionary Entrepreneurship: Building a Future through Purposeful Innovation", is written to inspire and guide entrepreneurs who want to build businesses that create a better future for themselves and for society as a whole. In this book, I explore the essential principles of visionary entrepreneurship and how they can be applied to create purposeful and innovative businesses that address real -world problems and create lasting positive change.

I begin by defining what I mean by "Visionay Entrepreneurship" and why I believe it is essential for entrepreneurs today to embrace this approach. I then explore the key elements of purposeful innovation, including the importance of creating a clear mission, understanding customer needs and developing sustainable business models. Throughout the book, I provide real-world examples of successful entrepreneurs who have built purposeful, innovative businesses and the strategies they have used to achieve their goals.

My aim in writing this book is to inspire and guide entrepreneurs who want to create businesses that are not only profitable but also make a positive impact on the world. Whether you are a seasoned entrepreneur or just starting, I believe that the principles of visionary entrepreneurship can help you build a better future for yourself, your team, your customers, your investors and society as a whole.

INTRODUCTION

Visionary Entrepreneurship is a concept that combines the power of imagination, innovation and entrepreneurship to build a future through purposeful innovation.
In today's rapidly changing business environment, visionary entrepreneurship is more important than ever for companies to stay competitive and succeed.

This Book, "Visionary Entrepreneurship : Building a Furure through Purposeful Innovation", aims to provide readers with the knowledge, tools and strategies necessary to become a visionary entrepreneur. The book will explore the core principles of visionary entrepreneurship including developing a clear and compelling vision, creating a culture of innovation, identifying emerging technologies, building strong partnerships and collaborations and mitigating potential risks associated with rapid growth.

Whether you are an aspiring entrepreneur, a seasoned business leader or simply someone interested in the future of innovation and entrepreneurship, this book is for you.

As we navigate through the challenges and opportunities of the 21st century, it is becoming increasingly clear that traditional business models and approaches are no longer sufficient. The world is changing rapidly and so must our mindset and actions towards entrepreneurship. Visionary Entrepreneurship is the answer to this call for change.

In this book, I will share my insights and experiences as an entrepreneur, innovator and the change maker to help you become a visionary entrepreneur. Together, we will explore the essential principles of visionary entrepreneurship and how they can be applied to create purposeful and innovative businesses that address real-world problems and create lasting positive change.

I believe that anyone can become a visionary entrepreneur. It doesn't matter where you come from , what your background is or how much experience you have. All that matters is your passion, your willingness to learn and your commitment to making a difference.

Through this book, I hope to inspire and guide you on your journey towards becoming a visionary entrepreneur. So, let's dive in and start building a better future through purposeful innovation.

"VISIONARY ENTREPRENEURSHIP: BUILDING A FUTURE THROUGH PURPOSEFUL INNOVATION."

"Commit your work to the Lord, and your plans will be established." - Proverbs 16:3

Welcome to "Visionary Entrepreneurship: Building a Future through Purposeful Innovation." This book is dedicated to entrepreneurs, innovators, and business leaders who are passionate about creating a better future through purposeful and sustainable innovation.

In today's rapidly changing world, entrepreneurship has become a driving force for economic growth, job creation, and social impact. However, starting and scaling a successful business requires more than just a good idea and hard work. It requires a vision, a purpose, and a commitment to making a positive difference in the world.

This book explores the fundamental principles of visionary

entrepreneurship, providing insights and practical guidance for those who seek to build purpose-driven businesses that make a lasting impact. From ideation to execution, we'll explore the key stages of entrepreneurial journey, highlighting the opportunities and challenges that entrepreneurs face along the way.

We'll also discuss the role of innovation in creating a sustainable future, exploring the latest trends and technologies that are driving change in various industries. We'll examine the importance of purposeful innovation, and how it can be used to solve some of the world's most pressing challenges while creating new opportunities for growth and impact.

Finally, we'll delve into the mindset and values that are essential for visionary entrepreneurs, including a deep commitment to ethical leadership, social responsibility, and stakeholder engagement. We'll explore the importance of building a strong organizational culture, creating diverse and inclusive teams, and developing effective partnerships and collaborations that can help entrepreneurs achieve their goals.

Whether you're a seasoned entrepreneur or just starting out, this book will provide you with the inspiration, insights, and practical guidance you need to build a future through purposeful innovation. So, let's get started and explore the exciting world of visionary entrepreneurship!

1. DEVELOPING A CLEAR AND COMPELLING VISION

Helen Keller: "The only thing worse than being blind is having sight but no vision."

The first step to becoming a visionary entrepreneur is to develop a clear and compelling vision that guides your decisions and actions. This topic will explore the process of defining a vision, identifying core values, and setting long-term goals.

Developing a clear and compelling vision is crucial for any entrepreneur who wants to build a successful business. A vision is the foundation upon which a business is built and provides direction for decision-making, goal-setting, and strategy development. Without a clear vision, entrepreneurs can easily become distracted, lose focus, and make decisions that are not aligned with their long-term goals.

To develop a clear and compelling vision, entrepreneurs should begin by identifying their core values. Core values are the principles and beliefs that guide an entrepreneur's decision-making and behavior. They are the foundation upon which a business is built and should be reflected in all aspects of the business, including its products or services, marketing and branding, and customer interactions.

Once core values have been identified, entrepreneurs should define their vision for the future. A vision is a statement of what an entrepreneur wants to achieve in the long term. It should be inspiring, aspirational, and compelling, and should provide a clear sense of direction for the business.

When developing a vision, entrepreneurs should consider the following questions:

- What problem am I solving?
- What are my core values?
- What kind of impact do I want to have on the world?
- What kind of legacy do I want to leave behind?

The answers to these questions can help entrepreneurs define their vision and set long-term goals. It's important to note that a vision is not set in stone and can be revised as the business evolves and new opportunities arise.

In addition to developing a clear and compelling vision, entrepreneurs should also focus on building a strong team that shares their vision and core values. This requires effective communication, leadership skills, and the ability to motivate and inspire others. Entrepreneurs should also be open to feedback and willing to adapt their vision as needed to ensure that it remains relevant and achievable.

Overall, developing a clear and compelling vision is the first step to becoming a visionary entrepreneur. By identifying core values, defining a vision, and setting long-term goals, entrepreneurs can build a strong foundation for their business and ensure that their decisions and actions are aligned with their long-term vision.

a) Defining the Core Purpose and Mission of Your Business.

Defining the core purpose and mission of your business is a critical step in building a successful and sustainable enterprise. Without a clear sense of what your business stands for, what it aims to achieve, and how it will operate, it will be difficult to align stakeholders, build a strong team, or develop a strategy for growth. In this topic, I will explore the importance of defining the core purpose and mission of your business, and provide some guidance on how to develop a clear and compelling statement that will guide your organization's decisions and actions.

The Importance Of Purpose And Mission.

At the heart of every successful business is a clear sense of purpose and mission. The purpose defines why the business exists – its reason for being – while the mission sets out what the business aims to achieve, and how it will achieve it. Together, these elements provide a framework for decision-making, goal-setting, and performance management. They help to create a shared sense of direction among stakeholders, and ensure that everyone is aligned around a common goal.

A clear sense of purpose and mission can also be a powerful motivator for employees, customers, and investors. It gives them a reason to believe in the business, and to invest their time, money, and resources in its success. It can help to build a strong brand identity, and to create a sense of loyalty and trust among stakeholders.

Defining Your Purpose And Mission

Defining your purpose and mission requires a thoughtful and deliberate process. It requires an understanding of the needs and aspirations of your stakeholders, as well as an assessment of your organization's strengths, weaknesses, opportunities, and threats. Here are some steps you can take to develop a clear and compelling purpose and mission statement for your business:

1. Conduct a stakeholder analysis: Start by identifying the key stakeholders in your business – including customers, employees, investors, suppliers, and community members. Conduct a survey or focus group to gather insights into their needs, wants, and expectations, and use this information to inform your purpose and mission statement.

2. Define your core values: Identify the values that underpin your business – such as honesty, integrity, innovation, or social responsibility – and use them as a guide for decision-making. These values should reflect the beliefs and aspirations of your stakeholders, and should be embedded into your organization's culture and operations.

3. Identify your unique selling proposition: Determine what sets your business apart from others in your industry. This could be a unique product or service offering, a more efficient production process, a commitment to sustainability, or a highly engaged customer base. Use this information to inform your mission statement, and to differentiate your brand in the market.

4. Develop a long-term vision: Consider where you want your business to be in five, ten, or twenty years' time. What impact do you want to have on your industry, your customers, and the world at large? Use this vision to inform your purpose statement, and to provide a sense of direction for your organization.

5. Keep it simple and memorable: Your purpose and mission statements should be concise, clear, and memorable. Avoid jargon or technical terms, and use language that resonates with your stakeholders. Make sure that everyone in your organization can understand and articulate the statements, and use them as a touchstone for decision-making.

Examples Of Purpose And Mission Statements.

Purpose and mission statements are essential components of any organization's identity. They communicate the company's values, vision, and goals to its stakeholders, including employees, customers, and investors. Below are some examples of purpose and mission statements from various companies:

1.Tesla
Purpose: "To accelerate the world's transition to sustainable energy."
Mission: "To create the most compelling car company of the 21st century by driving the world's transition to electric vehicles."

2. Patagonia
Purpose: "We're in business to save our home planet."
Mission: "Build the best product, cause no unnecessary harm, use business to inspire and implement solutions to the environmental crisis."

3. Microsoft

Purpose: "Empower every person and every organization on the planet to achieve more."
Mission: "To empower every person and every organization on the planet to achieve more through our technology and innovation."

4. Google
Purpose: "To organize the world's information and make it universally accessible and useful."
Mission: "To organize the world's information and make it universally accessible and useful."

5. Airbnb
Purpose: "Belong anywhere."
Mission: "To help create a world where you can belong anywhere and where people can live in a place, instead of just traveling to it."

6. Warby Parker
Purpose: "To offer designer eyewear at a revolutionary price, while leading the way for socially conscious businesses."
Mission: "To offer designer eyewear at a revolutionary price, while leading the way for socially conscious businesses."

7. TOMS
Purpose: "To improve lives."
Mission: "To improve people's lives through business."

These purpose and mission statements reflect the core values and priorities of these companies. They demonstrate a commitment to social responsibility, innovation, and sustainability. A well-crafted purpose and mission statement can help a company build its brand and attract customers who share its values.

b) Setting SMART (Specific, Measurable, Attainable, Relevant and Time-bound) Goals.

Setting SMART (specific, measurable, attainable, relevant, and time-bound) goals is a key factor in achieving success in any personal or professional endeavor. The SMART framework provides a structure for setting objectives that are clear, realistic, and achievable, while also providing a roadmap for tracking progress and making adjustments as needed. In this topic, we will explore the importance of setting SMART goals, and provide some guidance on how to develop goals that will help you achieve your desired outcomes.

The Importance Of Setting Smart Goals

Setting SMART goals is important for a number of reasons. First and foremost, it provides clarity and focus. When you have a clear and specific goal, you can direct your efforts towards achieving it, rather than wasting time and energy on tasks that are not relevant to your desired outcome. It also allows you to measure progress and make adjustments as needed, which can help you stay motivated and engaged.

Setting SMART goals also helps to ensure that your objectives are realistic and achievable. By breaking down your larger goals into smaller, more manageable tasks, you can create a sense of momentum and progress, which can help you stay on track and avoid getting overwhelmed. Additionally, setting SMART goals can help you identify potential roadblocks or challenges, and develop strategies for overcoming them.

The SMART Framework

The SMART framework consists of five key elements that should be included in any goal-setting process:

1. Specific: The goal should be clear and specific, outlining exactly what you want to achieve. It should answer the questions: What do I want to accomplish? Why is this goal important? Who is involved? Where will it take place? When will it be achieved?

2. Measurable: The goal should be quantifiable, so that progress can be tracked and measured. This can be done by setting concrete metrics or benchmarks, such as a specific number of sales, a percentage increase in productivity, or a specific amount of weight loss.

3. Attainable: The goal should be achievable and realistic, taking into account your resources, skills, and abilities. It should challenge you, but not be so far out of reach that it becomes discouraging or demotivating.

4. Relevant: The goal should be relevant to your overall objectives and align with your values and priorities. It should be something that is important to you and that will have a meaningful impact on your life or work.

5. Time-bound: The goal should have a specific deadline or timeline for completion. This helps to create a sense of urgency and accountability, and ensures that progress is being made.

Developing Smart Goals.

To develop SMART goals, it is helpful to follow a structured process that includes the following steps:

1. Identify your overall objective: Start by identifying the larger goal or objective that you want to achieve. This could be a personal goal, such as losing weight or learning a new skill, or a professional goal, such as increasing sales or improving customer satisfaction.

2. Break it down into smaller, specific goals: Once you have identified your overall objective, break it down into smaller, more specific goals that are easier to measure and achieve. These goals should be specific, measurable, and time-bound.

    3. Evaluate your resources: Consider the resources, skills, and abilities that you have available to you, and determine whether your goals are achievable and realistic.

    4. Consider potential roadblocks: Identify potential roadblocks or challenges that could prevent you from achieving your goals, and develop strategies for overcoming them.

    5. Develop a plan: Create a detailed plan for achieving your goals, including specific actions and timelines for each step.

Examples Of Smart Goals

To illustrate how the SMART framework can be applied, here are some examples of SMART goals in various contexts:

    1. Personal Goal: "I will lose 10 pounds by December 31st by exercising for 30 minutes, 5 days a week, and reducing my daily calorie intake by 500 calories."

Specific: Losing 10 pounds, exercising for 30 minutes, 5 days a week, reducing daily calorie intake by 500 calories.

Measurable: The goal is to lose 10 pounds, which is a quantifiable metric.

Attainable: Exercising for 30 minutes and reducing calorie intake by 500 calories is achievable for most people.

Relevant: Losing weight is relevant to the individual's personal goal.

Time-bound: The goal has a specific deadline of December 31st.

    2. Business Goal: "Increase monthly sales revenue by 15% by the end of the quarter by launching a new marketing campaign and expanding our product line."

Specific: Increasing sales revenue by 15%, launching a new marketing campaign, and expanding the product line.

Measurable: Sales revenue can be quantified, and the goal is to increase it by 15%.

Attainable: The marketing campaign and product line expansion are feasible and can contribute to increased revenue.
Relevant: Increasing sales revenue is a relevant business objective.
Time-bound: The goal has a specific deadline of the end of the quarter.

3. *Academic Goal:* "Achieve a grade point average (GPA) of 3.5 or higher by the end of the semester by attending all lectures, completing all assignments, and studying for at least 2 hours every day."
Specific: Achieving a GPA of 3.5 or higher, attending all lectures, completing all assignments, and studying for at least 2 hours every day.
Measurable: GPA is a quantifiable metric, and the goal is to achieve a specific score.
Attainable: Attending lectures, completing assignments, and studying for 2 hours every day are realistic actions that can contribute to achieving the goal.
Relevant: Achieving a high GPA is a relevant academic objective.
Time-bound: The goal has a specific deadline of the end of the semester.

4. *Health Goal:* "Run a 5k race in under 30 minutes by the end of the year by following a structured training program and increasing running distance and intensity."
Specific: Running a 5k race in under 30 minutes, following a structured training program, and increasing running distance and intensity.
Measurable: The goal is to run a 5k race in under 30 minutes, which is a quantifiable metric.
Attainable: Following a structured training program and gradually increasing running distance and intensity can lead to achieving the goal.
Relevant: Running a 5k race in under 30 minutes is a relevant health objective.

Time-bound: The goal has a specific deadline of the end of the year.

Conclusion

Setting SMART goals is an effective way to achieve success in personal and professional pursuits. By following the SMART framework, individuals can develop clear and specific goals that are achievable, relevant, and time-bound. SMART goals provide a roadmap for tracking progress and making adjustments as needed, which can help individuals stay motivated and engaged in their pursuits. Whether it's losing weight, increasing sales revenue, achieving academic success, or improving physical fitness, setting SMART goals is an important step towards achieving desired outcomes.

c) Identifying and Prioritizing Key Stakeholders.

Identifying and prioritizing key stakeholders is an important process for any organization or project. Stakeholders are individuals or groups who have a vested interest in the success or failure of the organization or project. Identifying and prioritizing stakeholders helps organizations and project teams understand who they need to engage, what their interests and expectations are, and how they can best manage stakeholder relationships to achieve their goals. In this section, we will discuss why identifying and prioritizing stakeholders is important, how to identify stakeholders, and how to prioritize them.

Why Identifying And Prioritizing Key Stakeholders Is Important.

Identifying and prioritizing key stakeholders is important for several reasons:

1.   **Effective stakeholder engagement:** Identifying and prioritizing key stakeholders helps organizations and project teams to engage with stakeholders more effectively. By understanding stakeholders' interests, needs, and expectations, organizations can tailor their communications and engagement strategies to meet stakeholders' needs and build positive relationships.

2.   **Managing stakeholder expectations:** Prioritizing stakeholders based on their level of influence and interest in the project helps organizations manage stakeholder expectations. By engaging with high-priority stakeholders early in the project, organizations can ensure that their interests and expectations are

taken into account.

3. **Mitigating risks:** Identifying and prioritizing stakeholders can help organizations to identify potential risks and opportunities associated with stakeholder relationships. By identifying stakeholders who may be opposed to the project or who may have competing interests, organizations can develop strategies to mitigate these risks and build support for the project.

4. **Achieving project success:** Effective stakeholder engagement is critical to achieving project success. By prioritizing stakeholders and engaging with them in a meaningful way, organizations can build support for the project and ensure that stakeholder interests are aligned with project goals.

How To Identify Key Stakeholders

Identifying key stakeholders involves a process of identifying all individuals and groups who may be impacted by the project or organization. This can include internal stakeholders, such as employees and management, as well as external stakeholders, such as customers, suppliers, regulators, and the community.

Here Are Some Steps To Follow When Identifying Stakeholders:

1. Conduct a stakeholder analysis:

A stakeholder analysis is a process of identifying all stakeholders who may be impacted by the project or organization. This involves identifying stakeholders' interests, needs, and expectations, as well as their level of influence and importance to the project or organization.

2. Brainstorm stakeholders:

Brainstorming is a useful tool for identifying stakeholders. Gather a group of individuals who have knowledge of the project or organization and brainstorm all individuals and groups who may be impacted by the project or organization. It is important to consider both internal and external stakeholders, as well as stakeholders who may have competing interests or may be opposed to the project.

3. Use stakeholder mapping tools:

Stakeholder mapping tools can help to identify stakeholders and their level of influence and importance to the project or organization. These tools typically involve creating a matrix with stakeholders listed on one axis and their level of influence and importance listed on the other axis.

4. Conduct research:

Conducting research can help to identify stakeholders who may not be immediately obvious. This can involve reviewing regulatory filings, media reports, and other public information sources to identify stakeholders who may be impacted by the project or organization.

How to Prioritize Key Stakeholders

Once stakeholders have been identified, it is important to prioritize them based on their level of influence and importance to the project or organization. Here are some steps to follow when prioritizing stakeholders:

1. Identify stakeholder influence: Identify stakeholders who have a high level of influence over the project or organization.

These stakeholders may include senior management, board members, regulators, and other individuals or groups who have decision-making power.

2. Identify stakeholder importance: Identify stakeholders who are important to the success of the project or organization. These stakeholders may include customers, suppliers, investors, employees, and other individuals or groups who have a direct or indirect impact on the organization.

3. Assess stakeholder interest: Assess stakeholders' level of interest in the project or organization. This can be done by reviewing stakeholder communications, attending stakeholder meetings, and conducting surveys or interviews.

4. Categorize stakeholders: Once stakeholders have been identified and assessed, categorize them into groups based on their level of influence and importance. For example, high-priority stakeholders may be those who have a high level of influence and importance, while low-priority stakeholders may be those who have a lower level of influence and importance.

5. Develop a stakeholder engagement plan: Once stakeholders have been prioritized, develop a stakeholder engagement plan that outlines how the organization will engage with each stakeholder group. This may include regular communications, meetings, and other engagement activities that are tailored to each stakeholder group's interests and needs.

6. Continuously monitor and update stakeholder priorities: Stakeholder priorities can change over time, so it is important to continuously monitor and update stakeholder priorities as needed. This may involve conducting regular stakeholder assessments, reviewing stakeholder communications, and staying up-to-date on changes in the external environment that may impact stakeholder priorities.

By prioritizing stakeholders based on their level of influence and importance, organizations can focus their resources on engaging with high-priority stakeholders and managing stakeholder relationships in a way that supports project or organizational success. Effective stakeholder engagement is a key driver of organizational success, and prioritizing stakeholders is an important step in achieving that success.

d) Creating a Values Statement to Guide Decision-Making.

A values statement is a powerful tool that can help guide decision-making within an organization. It articulates the core values and principles that the organization holds dear, and serves as a touchstone for decision-making, goal-setting, and behavior.

Here are some steps to follow when creating a values statement:

1. Conduct a values assessment: Before creating a values statement, it is important to conduct a values assessment to identify the values and principles that are most important to the organization. This can be done through surveys, focus groups, and other feedback mechanisms that allow stakeholders to share their opinions on what values are most important to the organization.

2. Identify key themes: Once values have been identified, look for common themes that emerge. For example, the organization may value honesty, integrity, and transparency, which could be grouped together under the theme of "ethics." Similarly, the organization may value innovation, creativity, and risk-taking, which could be grouped together under the theme of "entrepreneurship."

3. Draft the values statement: Using the themes that have emerged, draft a values statement that clearly articulates the values and principles that the organization holds dear. The statement should be concise and memorable, and should be easy for stakeholders to understand and remember.

4. Test the values statement: Once the values statement has been drafted, test it with stakeholders to ensure that it resonates with them and accurately reflects the organization's values. This may involve conducting focus groups or surveys to gather feedback on the statement.

5. Incorporate the values statement into decision-making: Once the values statement has been finalized, incorporate it into decision-making processes within the organization. This may involve training employees on the values statement, using it as a guide when setting goals and making decisions, and ensuring that all stakeholders understand and embrace the values statement.

Creating a values statement can be a powerful way to align an organization's culture, strategy, and behavior around a shared set of principles and values. When used effectively, a values statement can help guide decision-making, promote ethical behavior, and build a strong organizational culture that supports long-term success.

e) Building a Visual Representation of Your Vision, such as a Mission Statement or Vision Board.

Building a visual representation of your vision can be a powerful way to clarify your goals, motivate your team, and communicate your vision to others. Two popular ways to visually represent your vision are through a mission statement and a vision board.

Here is a closer look at each of these methods:

Mission Statement:

A mission statement is a concise statement that articulates an organization's purpose and values. It serves as a guidepost for decision-making and goal-setting, and helps align an organization's strategy and behavior around a shared vision. To create a mission statement, follow these steps:

1. Clarify your vision: Before crafting a mission statement, it is important to clarify your vision for the organization. What are your goals and aspirations? What impact do you want to have on the world? What values and principles are most important to you?

2. Identify your unique value proposition: Once your vision is clear, identify your unique value proposition. What sets your organization apart from others? What do you do better than anyone else? What is your competitive advantage?

3. Write a draft mission statement: Using your vision and unique value proposition as a guide, draft a concise and memorable mission statement. The statement should be no more than a sentence or two, and should clearly articulate your purpose and values.

4. *Refine your mission statement:* Once you have a draft mission statement, refine it by getting feedback from others and iterating on the wording until it is clear, concise, and memorable.

5. *Use your mission statement:* Once your mission statement is final, use it as a guidepost for decision-making, goal-setting, and communication. Incorporate it into your marketing materials, share it with your team, and use it as a touchstone when making decisions.

Vision Board:

A vision board is a visual representation of your goals and aspirations. It is typically created by gathering images, words, and other visual elements that represent your vision, and arranging them on a board or other medium in a way that is visually appealing and meaningful to you.

To create a vision board, follow these steps:

1. Clarify your vision:
Like with a mission statement, it is important to clarify your vision before creating a vision board. What are your goals and aspirations? What impact do you want to have on the world? What values and principles are most important to you?

2. Gather visual elements:
Once your vision is clear, gather visual elements that represent your vision. These can include images, words, phrases, and other visual elements that resonate with you and represent your goals and aspirations.

3. Arrange your visual elements:
Once you have gathered your visual elements, arrange them on a board or other medium in a way that is visually appealing and meaningful to you. You can organize your elements thematically,

chronologically, or in any other way that makes sense to you.

4. Display your vision board:

Once your vision board is complete, display it in a prominent location where you will see it often. Use it as a source of motivation and inspiration, and revisit it periodically to see if your goals and aspirations have changed.

Building a visual representation of your vision can be a powerful way to clarify your goals, motivate your team, and communicate your vision to others. Whether you choose to create a mission statement, a vision board, or other visual representation, the key is to stay true to your vision and use it as a guidepost for decision-making, goal-setting, and behavior.

2. CREATING A CULTURE OF INNOVATION

"Innovation distinguishes between a leader and a follower." - Steve Jobs

To build a future through purposeful innovation, visionary entrepreneurs must create a culture that fosters creativity, experimentation, and risk-taking. In today's fast-paced and ever-changing business environment, it is crucial to stay ahead of the curve and continuously innovate to meet the needs and demands of customers. This requires not only cutting-edge technology and strategic planning but also a workforce that is capable of ideation and implementation.

Establishing an innovative culture within an organization can be challenging, but there are several strategies that can be employed to encourage creativity and risk-taking. The first step is to hire employees who are not only skilled in their respective fields but also possess a passion for innovation and a willingness to take risks. This can be done by incorporating unconventional interview questions or challenges to assess a candidate's ability to think outside the box.

Training is another key component of building an innovative culture. Providing ongoing training and development opportunities can help employees stay up-to-date on the latest trends and technologies, as well as encourage them to explore new ideas and approaches. Additionally, mentorship programs can pair seasoned professionals with newer employees, allowing for knowledge sharing and collaboration.

Motivating employees is also critical to fostering an innovative culture. Providing incentives and recognition for creative ideas and successful innovation can help inspire employees to think outside the box and take calculated risks. Encouraging a positive work-life balance and providing a supportive work environment can also help employees feel empowered to explore new ideas and approaches.

In conclusion, building a future through purposeful innovation requires a culture that fosters creativity, experimentation, and risk-taking. Establishing such a culture requires strategic hiring, ongoing training, and development, and a supportive work environment. By following these strategies, visionary entrepreneurs can create an innovative workforce that is capable of driving growth and success in the future.

In this topic we will explore how to establish an innovative culture within an organization, including strategies for hiring, training, and motivating employees.

a) Encouraging Creativity and Idea Generation.

C reativity and idea generation are critical components of innovation and business success. Encouraging creativity and idea generation in your team can help to increase productivity, improve problem-solving, and foster a culture of innovation.

Here Are Some Strategies For Encouraging Creativity And Idea Generation In Your Team:

1. Create a Safe Environment for Idea Sharing:

One of the biggest obstacles to idea generation is fear of rejection or criticism. To encourage creativity, it is important to create a safe environment where team members feel comfortable sharing their ideas. This can be achieved by establishing ground rules for brainstorming sessions, such as no criticism or judgement of ideas during the ideation phase, and focusing on quantity of ideas over quality at first.

2. Use Brainstorming Techniques:

Brainstorming is a technique that can be used to generate a large number of ideas quickly. There are several types of brainstorming techniques, including traditional brainstorming, brainwriting, and mind mapping. Traditional brainstorming involves a group of people coming together to generate ideas, while brainwriting involves individuals writing down their ideas independently and then sharing them with the group. Mind mapping involves visually organizing ideas in a hierarchical way.

3. Encourage Divergent Thinking:

Divergent thinking is the ability to generate a variety of ideas and solutions to a problem. Encouraging divergent thinking can help to spark creativity and generate new ideas. This can be achieved by asking open-ended questions, challenging assumptions, and encouraging team members to think outside the box.

4. Provide Inspiration and Exposure to New Ideas:

Providing inspiration and exposure to new ideas can help to stimulate creativity and idea generation. This can be achieved by exposing team members to new experiences, attending conferences or workshops, or bringing in outside experts to speak to the team. Additionally, providing access to resources such as books, podcasts, and online courses can help to stimulate new ideas.

5. Foster Collaboration and Cross-functional Teams:

Collaboration and cross-functional teams can help to bring together diverse perspectives and skills, which can lead to more creative and innovative solutions. Encouraging collaboration can be achieved by creating opportunities for team members to work together on projects or tasks, and by facilitating communication and idea sharing across departments and teams.

6. Celebrate Creativity and Innovation:

Celebrating creativity and innovation can help to reinforce the importance of idea generation and encourage team members to continue thinking creatively. This can be achieved by recognizing and rewarding team members for their contributions, showcasing successful projects and ideas, and highlighting the benefits of innovation to the organization.

7. Embrace Failure:

Failure is a natural part of the innovation process, and can often lead to valuable learning and insights. Embracing failure and encouraging team members to take risks can help to foster a culture of innovation and creativity. This can be achieved by recognizing and celebrating failed ideas and projects, and encouraging team members to learn from their mistakes.

Encouraging creativity and idea generation can help to drive innovation and business success. By creating a safe environment for idea sharing, using brainstorming techniques, encouraging divergent thinking, providing inspiration and exposure to new ideas, fostering collaboration, celebrating creativity and innovation, and embracing failure, you can help to foster a culture of creativity and innovation in your team.

b) Providing Resources and Support for Experimentation.

Experimentation is an essential component of innovation and business success. It involves trying out new ideas, approaches, and strategies to see what works best. However, experimentation can be risky, and many organizations are reluctant to invest time and resources into something that may not yield immediate results. Providing resources and support for experimentation can help to overcome these barriers and foster a culture of innovation within your organization.

Here Are Some Strategies For Providing Resources And Support For Experimentation:

1. Allocate Time and Resources:

One of the most important resources for experimentation is time. Allowing team members dedicated time to experiment with new ideas and approaches can help to encourage innovation and creativity. In addition to time, providing resources such as funding, technology, and other necessary tools can help to support experimentation and increase the likelihood of success.

2. Establish a Culture of Experimentation:

Creating a culture of experimentation can help to normalize the process of trying new things and taking risks. This can be achieved by celebrating successes and learning from failures, encouraging open communication and idea sharing, and emphasizing the importance of experimentation in driving innovation and business success.

3. Encourage Prototyping and Testing:

Prototyping and testing can help to reduce the risk of experimentation by allowing team members to test out new ideas in a controlled environment before launching them to the broader organization or market. Encouraging prototyping and testing can help to identify and address potential issues early on in the process and increase the likelihood of success.

4. Provide Access to Training and Support:

Providing access to training and support can help to build the skills and knowledge necessary for successful experimentation. This can include training on design thinking, agile methodologies, and other innovation frameworks, as well as mentorship and coaching from experienced innovators within the organization.

5. Establish Metrics and Evaluation Criteria:

Establishing metrics and evaluation criteria can help to measure the success of experimentation and identify areas for improvement. This can include both quantitative and qualitative measures, such as revenue growth, customer satisfaction, and employee engagement. It is important to establish these metrics and evaluation criteria before launching an experiment to ensure that success is clearly defined.

6. Celebrate Successes and Learn from Failures:

Celebrating successes and learning from failures can help to reinforce the importance of experimentation and encourage continued innovation. Recognizing and rewarding successful experiments can help to build momentum and encourage others to take risks. Learning from failures can help to identify areas for improvement and guide future experimentation.

7. Empower Team Members:

Empowering team members to take ownership of experiments can help to build a sense of ownership and accountability. This can be achieved by providing autonomy and flexibility in how experiments are conducted, encouraging team members to take risks and try new approaches, and providing opportunities for feedback and input.

Providing resources and support for experimentation can help to drive innovation and business success. By allocating time and resources, establishing a culture of experimentation, encouraging prototyping and testing, providing access to training and support, establishing metrics and evaluation criteria, celebrating successes and learning from failures, and empowering team members, you can help to foster a culture of experimentation within your organization.

c) Promoting a Growth Mindset Among Employees.

A growth mindset is a powerful tool for personal and professional development. It is the belief that intelligence and abilities can be developed through dedication and hard work. Employees with a growth mindset are more likely to take on challenges, persevere through setbacks, and ultimately achieve greater success. As a business leader, it is important to promote a growth mindset among your employees.

Here Are Some Strategies For Doing So:

1. Provide Opportunities for Learning and Development:

Providing opportunities for learning and development can help to foster a growth mindset among employees. This can include training, mentorship, coaching, and other forms of professional development. Encouraging employees to take on new challenges and learn new skills can help them to build confidence and resilience.

2. Encourage Risk-Taking and Innovation:

Encouraging risk-taking and innovation can help to foster a growth mindset among employees. This can be achieved by creating a culture that celebrates experimentation and learning from failure. Encouraging employees to take calculated risks and try new approaches can help them to build resilience and adaptability.

3. Set Realistic Goals and Provide Support:

Setting realistic goals and providing support can help to promote a growth mindset among employees. Goals should be challenging but achievable, and employees should be provided with the necessary resources and support to achieve them. This can help employees to build confidence and develop a sense of accomplishment.

4. *Provide Regular Feedback:*

Providing regular feedback can help to promote a growth mindset among employees. Feedback should be specific, constructive, and focused on areas for improvement. It should also be delivered in a way that encourages employees to view it as an opportunity for growth and development, rather than criticism.

5. *Emphasize the Importance of Effort:*

Emphasizing the importance of effort can help to promote a growth mindset among employees. Employees should be encouraged to focus on their efforts and the process of learning, rather than just the outcome. This can help them to develop a sense of resilience and persistence in the face of challenges.

6. *Model a Growth Mindset:*

Modeling a growth mindset can be one of the most powerful ways to promote it among employees. As a business leader, you should demonstrate a commitment to learning and development, and a willingness to take on new challenges and learn from failure. This can help to create a culture that values growth and development

7. *Recognize and Celebrate Achievements:*

Recognizing and celebrating achievements can help to promote a growth mindset among employees. Employees should be recognized for their efforts and accomplishments, and encouraged to view their successes as a result of their hard work and dedication. This can help to reinforce the belief that abilities and intelligence can be developed through effort.

Promoting a growth mindset among employees can help to build a culture of learning and development within your organization. By providing opportunities for learning and development, encouraging risk-taking and innovation, setting realistic goals and providing support, providing regular feedback, emphasizing the importance of effort, modeling a growth mindset, and recognizing and celebrating achievements, you can help your employees to develop the mindset and skills necessary for personal and professional growth.

d) Encouraging Collaboration and Teamwork.

Collaboration and teamwork are essential to the success of any organization. When employees work together effectively, they can achieve greater results than when working independently. As a business leader, it is important to encourage collaboration and teamwork among your employees.

Here Are Some Strategies For Doing So:

1.   Foster a Collaborative Culture:
Fostering a collaborative culture is essential to encouraging collaboration and teamwork among employees. This can be achieved by creating an environment that encourages open communication, respect, and mutual support. Encouraging collaboration in your workplace can help to create a sense of community and teamwork, and foster a positive work culture.

2.   Set Clear Goals and Expectations:
Setting clear goals and expectations can help to promote collaboration and teamwork among employees. Clear goals and expectations can help employees understand what is expected of them and what they are working towards. This can help to align individual efforts with the goals of the organization and encourage collaboration towards a common goal.

3.   Create Opportunities for Collaboration:
Creating opportunities for collaboration can help to foster a sense of teamwork among employees. This can include group projects, team-building activities, brainstorming sessions, and other collaborative work. By creating opportunities for collaboration,

employees can learn from each other and develop new skills, which can ultimately benefit the organization as a whole.

4. *Encourage Open Communication:*

Encouraging open communication can help to promote collaboration and teamwork among employees. When employees feel comfortable sharing their thoughts and ideas with their colleagues, they are more likely to collaborate and work together effectively. Encouraging open communication can also help to prevent misunderstandings and improve problem-solving.

5. *Provide the Necessary Resources:*

Providing the necessary resources can help to facilitate collaboration and teamwork among employees. This can include tools and technology that enable remote collaboration, meeting spaces, and other resources that support collaboration. By providing the necessary resources, you can help to remove barriers to collaboration and ensure that employees have what they need to work together effectively.

6. *Recognize and Celebrate Achievements:*

Recognizing and celebrating achievements can help to promote collaboration and teamwork among employees. When employees feel that their contributions are valued, they are more likely to collaborate and work together effectively. By recognizing and celebrating achievements, you can help to create a sense of community and teamwork among employees.

7. *Foster Trust and Respect:*

Fostering trust and respect is essential to encouraging collaboration and teamwork among employees. Employees are more likely to collaborate when they feel that they can trust and respect their colleagues. This can be achieved by creating a culture that values transparency, honesty, and integrity. By fostering trust and respect, you can help to create a collaborative work environment that encourages teamwork.

8.   Provide Training and Development:

Providing training and development opportunities can help to promote collaboration and teamwork among employees. This can include team-building exercises, leadership training, and other forms of professional development that support collaboration and teamwork. By providing training and development opportunities, you can help employees develop the skills and knowledge necessary to work effectively with their colleagues.

9.   Lead by Example:

Leading by example is one of the most effective ways to encourage collaboration and teamwork among employees. As a business leader, you should model the behaviors and attitudes that you want to see in your employees. By demonstrating a commitment to collaboration and teamwork, you can help to create a culture that values these qualities.

Encouraging collaboration and teamwork among employees can help to foster a positive work environment and improve the overall success of your organization. By fostering a collaborative culture, setting clear goals and expectations, creating opportunities for collaboration, encouraging open communication, providing the necessary resources, recognizing and celebrating achievements, fostering trust and respect, providing training and development, and leading by example, you can create a work environment that promotes collaboration and teamwork among employees.

e) Celebrating Successes and Learning from Failures.

Successes and failures are a natural part of any business or organization. While it is easy to celebrate success, learning from failures is equally important to the growth and development of an organization. As a business leader, it is important to create a culture that celebrates successes and learns from failures.

Here Are Some Strategies For Doing So:

1. Celebrate Successes:

Celebrating successes is an important part of creating a positive work environment. Recognizing the accomplishments of employees can help to foster a sense of pride and motivation among team members. Celebrating successes can also help to reinforce positive behaviors and accomplishments. This can be done through team celebrations, recognition programs, or other forms of acknowledgment.

*2.   Encourage Learning from Failures:*While it is easy to focus on successes, learning from failures is equally important to the growth and development of an organization. Encouraging a culture that views failures as opportunities for growth and learning can help to foster resilience and innovation. Employees should be encouraged to share their experiences and reflect on what went wrong, why it went wrong, and how it can be prevented in the future.

3.   Create a Safe Environment:

Creating a safe environment is crucial for learning from failures.

Employees should feel comfortable sharing their failures without fear of repercussions or judgment. Creating a safe environment can help to foster a culture of trust, openness, and honesty. This can be done by creating policies that protect employees who speak up about failures, fostering an open-door policy, and encouraging feedback.

4. Analyze the Causes of Failure:

Analyzing the causes of failure can help to identify areas that need improvement. It can also help to prevent similar failures in the future. Conducting a root cause analysis can help to identify the underlying causes of the failure. This can be done by asking questions such as, "what went wrong?" and "why did it go wrong?".

5. Implement Changes:

Learning from failures is only effective if changes are implemented. After identifying the causes of failure, it is important to develop an action plan to address the underlying issues. This can include changes to processes, policies, or procedures. It is important to communicate these changes to employees and provide the necessary resources and support to implement them.

6. Share Successes and Failures:

Sharing successes and failures can help to foster a culture of transparency and openness. Sharing successes can help to reinforce positive behaviors and accomplishments, while sharing failures can help to identify areas that need improvement. Regularly communicating successes and failures can help to keep employees informed and engaged.

7. Learn from Other Organizations:

Learning from other organizations can provide valuable insights into how to celebrate successes and learn from failures. It can also help to identify best practices and strategies for improving performance. Networking with other business leaders, attending industry conferences, and reading industry publications can provide valuable insights and ideas.

Celebrating successes and learning from failures is essential to the growth and development of an organization. By celebrating successes, encouraging learning from failures, creating a safe environment, analyzing the causes of failure, implementing changes, sharing successes and failures, and learning from other organizations, business leaders can create a culture that fosters innovation, resilience and growth.

3. LEVERAGING EMERGING TECHNOLOGIES

"Technology is anything that wasn't around when you were born." - Alan Kay. *This quote highlights the ever-evolving nature of technology and the need for entrepreneurs to stay updated and leverage emerging technologies to remain competitive in the market.*

In today's fast-paced business world, technology is one of the most significant driving forces of innovation and growth. The world is constantly evolving, and visionary entrepreneurs must stay ahead of the curve to remain competitive. These entrepreneurs need to be aware of emerging technologies and have the ability to identify and leverage them to create new products, services, and business models.

To start, entrepreneurs need to keep an eye on emerging technologies and trends, such as artificial intelligence, blockchain, and the Internet of Things (IoT). These technologies have the potential to disrupt traditional business models and open up new opportunities for innovation. By staying informed and aware of these emerging technologies, entrepreneurs can begin to explore how they can be leveraged to create new value for their customers.

Once entrepreneurs have identified a promising technology, they need to determine how it can be integrated into their existing business model or used to create a new one. This may involve investing in research and development, hiring experts in the field, or partnering with technology providers or startups. In some cases, entrepreneurs may need to build entirely new teams or departments to handle the development and implementation of the new technology.

Entrepreneurs must also ensure that they have the necessary resources and infrastructure to support the technology. This may include upgrading existing IT systems, investing in new equipment or software, or hiring additional staff to manage the new technology.

Finally, entrepreneurs need to be willing to take risks and experiment with new ideas. They must be willing to embrace failure as a learning opportunity and pivot quickly if their ideas don't work out. Building a culture of experimentation and risk-taking is essential for entrepreneurs who want to stay ahead of the curve and create innovative solutions that meet the needs of their customers.

In summary, visionary entrepreneurs must be proactive in identifying and leveraging emerging technologies to stay competitive and build a future through purposeful innovation. They need to keep a pulse on emerging trends, integrate new technologies into their existing business model, ensure they have the necessary resources and infrastructure to support the technology, and foster a culture of experimentation and risk-taking within their organization.

In this topic, we will explore how to identify and leverage emerging technologies to create new products, services, and business models.

a) Conducting Ongoing Research on Emerging Technologies.

In today's fast-paced business environment, keeping up with emerging technologies is essential for staying competitive. Conducting ongoing research on emerging technologies can help businesses to identify new opportunities, improve processes, and gain a competitive advantage.

Here Are Some Strategies For Conducting Ongoing Research On Emerging Technologies:

1. Identify Relevant Technologies:

The first step in conducting ongoing research on emerging technologies is to identify which technologies are relevant to your business. This can be done by monitoring industry publications, attending industry conferences, and networking with other business leaders. It is important to focus on technologies that have the potential to impact your business, rather than just following the latest trends.

2. Allocate Resources:

Conducting ongoing research on emerging technologies requires time, resources, and expertise. Allocating resources to technology research can help to ensure that your business stays up-to-date with the latest trends and innovations. This can include investing in technology research tools, hiring technology experts, or partnering with technology vendors.

3. Establish a Research Plan:

Establishing a research plan can help to ensure that your technology research efforts are focused and effective. This can include setting goals, identifying research methods, and allocating resources. It is important to establish a regular schedule for technology research, such as weekly or monthly updates.

4. Monitor Industry Trends:

Monitoring industry trends can help to identify emerging technologies and stay ahead of the curve. This can include monitoring industry publications, attending industry conferences, and networking with other business leaders. It is important to stay abreast of industry trends to identify new opportunities and gain a competitive advantage.

5. Conduct Market Research:

Conducting market research can help to identify emerging technologies and assess their potential impact on your business. This can include conducting surveys, focus groups, and other research methods to gather insights from customers, employees, and other stakeholders. Market research can help to identify customer needs, preferences, and pain points, which can inform technology research efforts.

6. Build a Technology Roadmap:

Building a technology roadmap can help to prioritize technology research efforts and ensure that new technologies are integrated into business operations. A technology roadmap should identify key technologies, prioritize implementation, and establish timelines for implementation. This can help to ensure that new technologies are integrated into business operations in a way that maximizes their impact.

7. Monitor Competitors:

Monitoring competitors can help to identify emerging technologies that may be a threat to your business. This can include monitoring their technology investments, product releases, and market strategies. It is important to stay ahead of competitors by identifying emerging technologies and responding quickly to new threats.

8. Partner with Technology Vendors:

Partnering with technology vendors can provide access to expertise and resources that may not be available in-house. Technology vendors can provide insights into emerging technologies, as well as offer solutions for implementing and integrating new technologies into business operations. Partnering with technology vendors can help to ensure that your business stays up-to-date with the latest innovations and trends.

9. Establish a Technology Committee:

Establishing a technology committee can help to ensure that technology research efforts are aligned with business goals and objectives. A technology committee should include representatives from different business functions, such as marketing, operations, and IT. The committee can help to prioritize technology research efforts, identify opportunities for innovation, and provide oversight for technology investments.

10. Continuously Evaluate and Refine:

Conducting ongoing research on emerging technologies requires continuous evaluation and refinement. It is important to regularly evaluate the effectiveness of technology research efforts and refine strategies as needed. This can include adjusting research methods, reallocating resources, or pivoting in response to changing industry trends.

In conclusion, conducting ongoing research on emerging technologies is essential for staying competitive in today's fast-paced business environment. By identifying relevant technologies, allocating resources, establishing a research plan, monitoring industry trends, conducting market research, building a technology roadmap, monitoring competitors, partnering with technology vendors, establishing a technology committee and continuously evaluating and refining technology research efforts, businesses can stay ahead of the curve and build a future through purposeful innovation. This requires a commitment to ongoing learning and adaptation as well a willingness to take calculated risks and embrace new opportunities.

b) Experimenting with New Technologies to Identify Potential Use Cases.

Experimenting with new technologies is a key component of innovation and staying competitive in today's fast-paced business environment. Through experimentation, businesses can identify potential use cases for new technologies and determine how they can be applied to improve business operations, enhance customer experiences, and create new opportunities for growth.

Here Are Some Strategies For Experimenting With New Technologies To Identify Potential Use Cases:

1. Identify Business Challenges and Opportunities:
Before experimenting with new technologies, it is important to identify business challenges and opportunities that the technology can help to address. This can include identifying pain points in business operations, customer needs and preferences, and emerging market trends. By identifying these challenges and opportunities, businesses can focus their experimentation efforts and determine how the new technology can be applied to address them.

2. Research Emerging Technologies:
Researching emerging technologies is an important step in identifying potential use cases. This can include monitoring industry publications, attending technology conferences, and networking with other business leaders. By staying up-to-date with the latest technologies, businesses can identify new opportunities for innovation and determine which technologies are most relevant to their business.

3. Set Clear Objectives:

Setting clear objectives for experimentation is important to ensure that the process is focused and effective. This can include identifying specific business challenges or opportunities that the new technology can help to address, and defining key performance indicators (KPIs) to measure success. By setting clear objectives, businesses can determine whether the new technology is delivering the expected results and make adjustments as needed.

4. Start Small:

Starting small is important when experimenting with new technologies. This can include conducting small-scale tests to determine the feasibility of the technology and identify any potential challenges. By starting small, businesses can minimize risks and costs associated with experimentation and determine whether the technology has the potential to deliver the desired results.

5. Collaborate with Technology Vendors:

Collaborating with technology vendors is an important part of experimentation. Technology vendors can provide expertise and resources that may not be available in-house, including access to the latest technologies and solutions for integrating them into business operations. By collaborating with technology vendors, businesses can accelerate the experimentation process and ensure that the technology is being applied in the most effective way.

6. Involve Cross-Functional Teams:

Involving cross-functional teams is important to ensure that experimentation efforts are aligned with business goals and objectives. This can involve employees from different departments, such as marketing, operations, and IT. By involving cross-functional teams, businesses can gain a more holistic view of the potential use cases for the new technology and ensure that it is being applied in a way that maximizes its impact.

7. Gather Feedback from Stakeholders:

Gathering feedback from stakeholders is important to ensure that the new technology is meeting their needs and expectations. This can include gathering feedback from customers, employees, and other stakeholders through surveys, focus groups, and other research methods. By gathering feedback, businesses can identify any potential challenges or opportunities for improvement and make adjustments as needed.

8. Measure Results and Iterate:

Measuring results and iterating is an important part of the experimentation process. This can include measuring key performance indicators (KPIs) and using the data to refine the experimentation approach. By measuring results and iterating, businesses can determine whether the new technology is delivering the expected results and make adjustments as needed to optimize its impact.

9. Develop a Business Case:

Developing a business case is important to ensure that the new technology is being applied in a way that maximizes its return on investment (ROI). This can include identifying the costs and benefits associated with the technology and determining the potential impact on business operations, customer experiences, and revenue growth. By developing a business case, businesses can determine whether the new technology is a viable investment and justify its implementation to stakeholders.

Stay Up-To-Date:

Staying up-to-date with emerging technologies is crucial for businesses that want to remain competitive and innovative.

Here are some strategies for staying up-to-date:

1. Monitor Industry Publications:

Industry publications, such as magazines, journals, and online news sources, can provide valuable insights into emerging technologies and their potential impact on business. By regularly monitoring these publications, businesses can stay informed about the latest developments and trends in their industry.

2. Attend Technology Conferences:

Attending technology conferences is a great way to learn about new technologies and their potential applications. These conferences often feature keynote speakers, panel discussions, and workshops that provide valuable insights into emerging technologies and their impact on business.

3. Network with Other Business Leaders:

Networking with other business leaders can provide valuable insights into emerging technologies and their potential applications. This can include attending industry events and conferences, participating in online forums, and joining industry associations.

4. Partner with Technology Vendors:

Partnering with technology vendors can provide businesses with access to the latest technologies and expertise in their implementation. Technology vendors can provide insights into emerging technologies and help businesses determine how they can be applied to address specific business challenges and opportunities.

5. Conduct Research and Development:

Research and development (R&D) is a key component of staying up-to-date with emerging technologies. By investing in R&D, businesses can explore new technologies and their potential applications, and identify new opportunities for innovation and growth.

6. Establish an Innovation Culture:

Establishing an innovation culture within the organization can help to promote awareness and adoption of emerging technologies. This can include encouraging employees to explore new technologies and providing them with resources and support to experiment and innovate.

7. Hire Tech-Savvy Employees:

Hiring tech-savvy employees can help to ensure that businesses are aware of emerging technologies and their potential applications. These employees can bring valuable insights into emerging technologies and help to drive innovation within the organization.

8. Monitor Competitors:

Monitoring competitors can provide valuable insights into emerging technologies and their potential applications. By monitoring competitors, businesses can stay informed about the latest developments and trends in their industry and identify new opportunities for innovation and growth.

9.   Leverage Social Media:

Social media can be a valuable source of information on emerging technologies and their potential applications. By following relevant industry influencers and hashtags, businesses can stay informed about the latest developments and trends in their industry.

10.   Engage with Experts:

Engaging with experts, such as consultants and industry analysts, can provide valuable insights into emerging technologies and their potential applications. These experts can provide customized advice and recommendations on how to apply emerging technologies to address specific business challenges and opportunities.

Conclusion

In conclusion, staying up-to-date with emerging technologies is essential for businesses that want to remain competitive and innovative. By monitoring industry publications, attending technology conferences, networking with other business leaders, partnering with technology vendors, conducting research and development, establishing an innovation culture, hiring tech-savvy employees, monitoring competitors, leveraging social media, and engaging with experts, businesses can stay informed about the latest developments and trends in their industry and identify new opportunities for innovation and growth. By embracing emerging technologies and investing in research and development, businesses can position themselves for success in an increasingly technology-driven marketplace.

c) Collaborating with Experts in the Field to Stay Up-to-Date on New Developments.

Collaborating with experts in the field is one of the most effective ways for businesses to stay up-to-date on new developments. Experts bring a wealth of knowledge and experience to the table, and can provide valuable insights and advice on emerging trends and technologies. In this topic, we will explore the benefits of collaborating with experts and offer tips on how to establish and maintain successful collaborations.

Benefits Of Collaborating With Experts

1. Access to Specialized Knowledge and Expertise

Experts have specialized knowledge and expertise in a particular field or area, which can be extremely valuable to businesses looking to stay up-to-date on new developments. By collaborating with experts, businesses can gain insights into emerging trends and technologies, as well as access to cutting-edge research and development.

2. Opportunities for Networking and Partnership

Collaborating with experts can also provide businesses with opportunities for networking and partnership. Experts often have established networks within their industry or field, which can be leveraged by businesses looking to expand their reach and establish new partnerships.

3. Enhanced Decision-Making

By collaborating with experts, businesses can make more informed decisions about emerging trends and technologies.

Experts can provide objective assessments and evaluations of new developments, helping businesses to determine which technologies are most relevant and how they can be applied to achieve specific business goals.

4. Innovation and Creativity

Collaborating with experts can also increase innovation and creativity within the organization. Experts can provide fresh perspectives and ideas on emerging trends and technologies, inspiring new ways of thinking and approaching business challenges.

Tips For Collaborating With Experts

1. Identify the Right Experts

The first step in collaborating with experts is identifying the right experts to work with. This requires a thorough understanding of the business's needs and objectives, as well as an understanding of the expertise and capabilities of potential collaborators.

2. Establish Clear Goals and Objectives

Once the right experts have been identified, it is important to establish clear goals and objectives for the collaboration. This includes defining the scope of the collaboration, as well as outlining specific deliverables and timelines.

3. Foster Communication and Collaboration

Effective communication and collaboration are essential for successful collaborations with experts. This includes regular check-ins, clear communication channels, and opportunities for feedback and input from all parties involved.

4. Provide Adequate Resources and Support

Collaborating with experts often requires significant resources and support. This includes funding, personnel, and infrastructure, as well as access to data and research materials.

5. Establish Clear Roles and Responsibilities

Establishing clear roles and responsibilities for all parties involved is essential for ensuring a successful collaboration. This includes defining the responsibilities of the business and the expert, as well as outlining the expectations and deliverables for each party.

6. Foster a Culture of Innovation

Finally, it is important to foster a culture of innovation within the organization. This includes encouraging experimentation and risk-taking, as well as providing resources and support for innovation and creativity.

Conclusion

Collaborating with experts is an effective way for businesses to stay up-to-date on new developments and trends. By leveraging the specialized knowledge and expertise of experts, businesses can gain valuable insights into emerging technologies and trends, as well as access to cutting-edge research and development. To establish successful collaborations with experts, businesses should identify the right experts, establish clear goals and objectives, foster communication and collaboration, provide adequate resources and support, establish clear roles and responsibilities, and foster a culture of innovation. By following these tips, businesses can establish successful collaborations with experts and position themselves for success in an increasingly competitive marketplace.

d) Prioritizing Investments in Technologies that Align with Your Business Goals and Values.

In today's fast-paced business environment, companies are constantly evaluating and implementing new technologies to gain a competitive edge. While investing in new technologies can bring a lot of benefits, it's important to prioritize investments in technologies that align with your business goals and values. This ensures that your investments are directed towards solutions that are relevant and impactful, and that they support your overall mission and vision.

Here Are Some Key Considerations To Help Prioritize Investments In Technologies That Align With Your Business Goals And Values:

1. Identify Your Business Goals and Values

Before you can prioritize investments in technologies, you need to identify your business goals and values. This involves taking a deep dive into your company's mission statement, values, and strategic objectives. It's important to understand the core purpose of your business and what you hope to achieve in the short and long term. This helps you identify the key areas where technology can support your business goals.

For example, if your business values sustainability and reducing carbon emissions, you may want to prioritize investments in energy-efficient technologies and solutions that help you reduce your carbon footprint. On the other hand, if your business goal is to increase efficiency and productivity, you may want to focus on technologies that streamline your operations and automate manual processes.

2. Conduct a Technology Assessment

Once you've identified your business goals and values, the next step is to conduct a technology assessment. This involves taking stock of the technologies you currently have in place, evaluating their effectiveness, and identifying any gaps or areas for improvement.

During this assessment, it's important to consider factors such as the age and condition of your current technology infrastructure, the compatibility of your systems, and the potential risks associated with outdated or unsupported technologies. You should also evaluate how your existing technologies align with your business goals and values.

This assessment can help you identify which technologies are critical to your business operations and which ones can be replaced or phased out over time. It also helps you identify areas where new technologies can make a significant impact and drive value for your business.

3. Evaluate New Technologies

Once you've identified your business goals and values and conducted a technology assessment, you can start evaluating new technologies. This involves researching the latest trends and developments in your industry, attending trade shows and conferences, and seeking input from experts and vendors in the field.

It's important to evaluate each new technology in terms of how well it aligns with your business goals and values. This involves assessing its potential impact on your operations, its compatibility with your existing infrastructure, and its ability to address any gaps or areas for improvement identified in your technology assessment.

When evaluating new technologies, it's also important to consider factors such as cost, implementation timeline, and potential return on investment. This helps you prioritize your investments and ensures that you're directing your resources towards solutions that are likely to generate the greatest value for your business.

4. Build a Technology Roadmap

Once you've evaluated new technologies and identified those that align with your business goals and values, the next step is to build a technology roadmap. This involves creating a plan for how you will implement these technologies over time, taking into account factors such as budget, resource availability, and implementation timelines.

When building your technology roadmap, it's important to prioritize your investments based on the potential impact each technology will have on your business. This involves identifying which technologies will have the greatest impact on your operations and help you achieve your business goals, and directing your resources towards those solutions.

Your technology roadmap should also include plans for monitoring and evaluating the effectiveness of your new technologies over time. This helps you ensure that your investments are generating the desired outcomes and that you're continuously improving your technology infrastructure to support your business goals.

Overall, prioritizing investments in technologies that align with your business goals and values requires a strategic approach that takes into account a wide range of factors, including your industry, your customers, your competition, and your organizational culture. By staying up-to-date on emerging technologies, experimenting with new ideas, fostering a culture of innovation, and collaborating with experts in the field, you can ensure that your investments in technology are strategic, effective, and aligned with your overall business strategy.

e) Developing a Strategy for Implementing New Technologies into Your Business Operations.

Developing a strategy for implementing new technologies into your business operations can be a complex and challenging process, but it is crucial for staying competitive and meeting the changing needs of customers. With technology advancing rapidly, it can be difficult to keep up with new developments and determine which technologies are worth investing in. However, by developing a clear strategy, you can ensure that your investments in technology are aligned with your business goals and objectives, and that they will provide tangible benefits to your organization.

Here Are Some Key Steps For Developing A Strategy For Implementing New Technologies Into Your Business Operations:

1. Identify your business goals and objectives

Before you begin investing in new technologies, it's important to have a clear understanding of your business goals and objectives. What are the key areas where you need to improve efficiency or effectiveness? What are the biggest pain points for your customers or employees? By identifying these areas, you can begin to prioritize your investments in new technologies and focus on solutions that will provide the most value to your organization.

2. Conduct a technology audit

Once you have identified your business goals and objectives, it's important to conduct a technology audit to determine which areas of your business are in need of technological improvements. This audit should include an assessment of your current technology infrastructure, as well as an analysis of the technology trends and emerging technologies that could be relevant to your business.

3. Evaluate potential technologies

After conducting a technology audit, you should have a better understanding of the technologies that could potentially benefit your organization. It's important to evaluate these technologies based on factors such as cost, implementation time, potential benefits, and alignment with your business goals and values. You may also want to consider conducting pilot tests of the technology to evaluate its effectiveness and identify any potential issues or challenges.

4. Develop an implementation plan

Once you have identified the technologies that you want to implement, you need to develop a plan for how to roll them out across your organization. This plan should include details such as timelines, resource requirements, training needs, and potential risks or challenges. It's important to involve key stakeholders in the development of this plan to ensure that everyone is aligned and committed to the implementation process.

5. Execute the implementation plan

With your implementation plan in place, it's time to begin executing. This may involve installing new hardware or software, training employees on how to use the new technology, and making any necessary changes to your business processes to accommodate the new technology. It's important to closely monitor the implementation process to identify any issues or challenges, and to make adjustments as needed to ensure that the technology is being integrated effectively into your operations.

6. Measure and evaluate results

Once the new technology has been fully implemented, it's important to measure and evaluate its impact on your business operations. This may include metrics such as improved efficiency, increased productivity, or higher customer satisfaction ratings. By measuring the results of your technology investments, you can determine whether they have been successful and identify areas where further improvements may be needed.

7. Continuously evaluate and adapt

Finally, it's important to recognize that technology is constantly evolving, and that your strategy for implementing new technologies must be flexible and adaptable to keep up with these changes. This may involve regularly conducting technology audits, evaluating emerging technologies, and making adjustments to your implementation plan based on changing business needs or market conditions.

In conclusion, developing a strategy for implementing new technologies into your business operations is a critical component of staying competitive and meeting the changing needs of customers. By following the key steps outlined above, you can ensure that your investments in technology are aligned with your business goals and values, and that they provide tangible benefits to your organization.

4. BUILDING SUSTAINABLE BUSINESSES

"Sustainability is not a buzzword, it's a mindset. It's about taking responsibility for the impact of our actions on the planet and the people who live on it." - Anand Mahindra

Building a sustainable business is not just about being socially and environmentally responsible, but also about creating long-term value for all stakeholders involved. Visionary entrepreneurs understand this and recognize that prioritizing sustainability is crucial for their business success in the long run.

One key strategy for building a sustainable business is to incorporate sustainable practices into all aspects of the business, from sourcing materials to production processes, to the end product or service. This can involve utilizing renewable energy sources, reducing waste and emissions, and implementing eco-friendly packaging and delivery options.

Another strategy is to prioritize social responsibility by engaging in ethical and fair labor practices, supporting local communities, and contributing to social causes. By doing so, businesses can establish a positive reputation and build customer loyalty, while also making a positive impact on society.

In addition, visionary entrepreneurs can leverage sustainability as a competitive advantage by developing innovative solutions that address environmental and social challenges. For example, developing products that are made from recycled materials or using technology to reduce energy consumption can not only benefit the environment but also differentiate the business from competitors.

Overall, building a sustainable business requires a long-term perspective and a commitment to creating value for all stakeholders involved. By prioritizing sustainability, visionary entrepreneurs can not only drive business success but also make a positive impact on the world.

Visionary entrepreneurs recognize that sustainability is not just a buzzword, but a crucial element of long-term success. In this topic we will explore strategies for building businesses that are environmentally and socially responsible, and that prioritize long-term value creation over short-term profits.

a) Identifying Areas of Environmental and Social Impact Within Your Business.

Identifying areas of environmental and social impact within your business is crucial to ensuring sustainable and responsible operations. With increasing awareness and concern for environmental and social issues, consumers and stakeholders are demanding greater transparency and accountability from businesses. By identifying and addressing your business's impact, you can reduce negative effects on the environment and society, build a positive reputation, and create long-term value for your stakeholders.

Here Are Some Key Steps To Help You Identify Areas Of Environmental And Social Impact Within Your Business:

1. *Conduct a sustainability assessment:*

Start by conducting a sustainability assessment to identify the environmental and social impacts of your business. This assessment should include an analysis of your operations, products, and supply chain. Some key areas to focus on include energy use, greenhouse gas emissions, waste generation, water consumption, and social issues such as labor practices, human rights, and community impact. Use this assessment to identify areas of greatest impact and prioritize your efforts.

2. *Engage stakeholders:*

Engage your stakeholders, including employees, customers, suppliers, and community members, to gain insight into their expectations and concerns regarding your business's impact. This can help you identify areas that may not have been considered in your initial assessment and prioritize areas that are of most concern to your stakeholders.

3.   *Develop a sustainability strategy:*

Develop a sustainability strategy that outlines your goals, targets, and initiatives to address your business's impact. This should be aligned with your overall business strategy and should take into account your key stakeholders' expectations and concerns. Your strategy should also include a timeline for achieving your goals and targets.

4.   *Monitor and measure progress:*

It's important to monitor and measure your progress to ensure that your sustainability initiatives are effective and on track. Establish metrics and targets to measure your performance, and regularly report on your progress to your stakeholders. This can help you identify areas that require additional attention and ensure that you are meeting your commitments.

5.   *Collaborate with suppliers and partners:*

Work with your suppliers and partners to identify areas of environmental and social impact within your supply chain. Encourage them to adopt sustainable practices and work with them to address any issues that are identified. This can help you reduce your overall impact and create a more sustainable supply chain.

6.   *Continuously improve:*

Finally, it's important to continuously improve your sustainability initiatives. Stay up-to-date on new technologies and best practices, and incorporate them into your strategy as appropriate. Engage with your stakeholders to gain feedback and suggestions for improvement, and use this to refine and enhance your sustainability initiatives over time.

In conclusion, identifying areas of environmental and social impact within your business is crucial to ensuring sustainable and responsible operations. By conducting a sustainability assessment, engaging your stakeholders, developing a sustainability strategy, monitoring and measuring progress, collaborating with suppliers and partners, and continuously improving, you can reduce negative impacts on the environment and society, build a positive reputation, and create long-term value for your stakeholders.

b) Setting Targets for Reducing Your Carbon Footprint and Other Environmental Impacts.

As individuals and organizations alike become more aware of the pressing need to address climate change and other environmental issues, setting targets for reducing your carbon footprint and other environmental impacts is becoming increasingly important. Taking action to reduce your organization's environmental footprint not only helps to protect the planet, but can also help to improve your bottom line, enhance your reputation, and attract and retain customers who are concerned about the environment.

Here Are Some Key Steps You Can Take To Set Targets For Reducing Your Carbon Footprint And Other Environmental Impacts:

1. Assess your current environmental impacts:

Before you can set targets for reducing your environmental impacts, you need to understand what those impacts are. Conduct an assessment of your organization's environmental impacts, including its greenhouse gas emissions, energy use, water use, waste generation, and other relevant factors. This will help you identify areas where you can make the most significant reductions.

2. Set ambitious, science-based targets:

To truly make a meaningful impact on the environment, it's important to set targets that are both ambitious and based on scientific evidence. There are a number of organizations that can help you set science-based targets for reducing your carbon footprint, including the Science-Based Targets initiative and the UN Global Compact.

3. Develop a plan for achieving your targets:

Once you've set your targets, you need to develop a plan for achieving them. This may involve making changes to your business operations, such as switching to renewable energy sources, improving energy efficiency, reducing waste, or changing your supply chain practices. Be sure to involve key stakeholders in the development of your plan, including employees, customers, and suppliers.

4. Track your progress:

To ensure that you're making progress towards your targets, it's important to track your environmental impacts over time. This will allow you to identify areas where you're making progress and areas where you need to do more work. Use a combination of internal data collection and external reporting frameworks, such as the Global Reporting Initiative or the Carbon Disclosure Project, to track your progress and report on your environmental performance.

5. Communicate your progress:

Finally, it's important to communicate your progress towards your environmental targets to stakeholders both inside and outside of your organization. This will help to build support for your environmental initiatives and demonstrate your commitment to sustainability. Use a variety of communication channels, including social media, your website, and your annual sustainability report, to share your progress and engage with stakeholders.

By setting ambitious, science-based targets for reducing your carbon footprint and other environmental impacts, and developing a plan for achieving those targets, you can help to protect the planet, enhance your reputation, and build a more sustainable business for the future.

c) Developing Sustainable Supply Chain Practices.

In recent years, there has been increasing awareness of the environmental and social impact of supply chain practices. This has led to a growing trend towards developing sustainable supply chain practices. Companies are now looking to reduce their carbon footprint and improve their social and environmental impact by working with suppliers who share their values and are committed to sustainable practices.

Developing sustainable supply chain practices is a complex process that involves collaboration with suppliers, customers, and other stakeholders. It requires a long-term commitment to sustainability and a willingness to invest time and resources into making changes.

Here Are Some Key Steps That Companies Can Take To Develop Sustainable Supply Chain Practices:

1. Identify the key sustainability issues

The first step in developing sustainable supply chain practices is to identify the key sustainability issues that are relevant to your business. This will depend on the nature of your business and the products and services that you offer. For example, if you are a clothing manufacturer, your key sustainability issues might include water usage, energy consumption, and waste management.

2. Engage with suppliers

Once you have identified the key sustainability issues, you need to engage with your suppliers to understand their sustainability practices. This involves conducting audits and assessments of your suppliers to determine their level of compliance with your sustainability standards. It is also important to communicate your expectations to your suppliers and work with them to develop strategies for improving their sustainability practices.

3. Develop sustainability metrics

To measure the effectiveness of your sustainable supply chain practices, it is important to develop sustainability metrics. These metrics should be based on your key sustainability issues and should be aligned with your overall sustainability goals. Some examples of sustainability metrics include greenhouse gas emissions, water usage, waste reduction, and supplier compliance.

4. Integrate sustainability into your procurement process

To ensure that sustainability is a key consideration in your procurement process, it is important to integrate sustainability into your procurement policies and procedures. This involves developing sustainability criteria that suppliers must meet in order to be considered for procurement. You can also use sustainability metrics to evaluate suppliers and include sustainability requirements in your contracts with suppliers.

5. Collaborate with other stakeholders

Developing sustainable supply chain practices requires collaboration with other stakeholders, including customers, suppliers, and other partners. By working together, you can share best practices, identify opportunities for improvement, and develop strategies for addressing sustainability challenges.

6. Monitor and report progress

Finally, to ensure that your sustainable supply chain practices are effective, it is important to monitor and report on your progress. This involves collecting data on your sustainability metrics, tracking your performance against your targets, and reporting your progress to your stakeholders. It is also important to use this information to identify areas for improvement and develop strategies for making further progress towards your sustainability goals.

In conclusion, developing sustainable supply chain practices is a critical step towards reducing the environmental and social impact of your business operations. By engaging with suppliers, developing sustainability metrics, integrating sustainability into your procurement process, collaborating with other stakeholders, and monitoring and reporting your progress, you can develop sustainable supply chain practices that align with your business goals and values.

d) Creating a Culture of Corporate Social Responsibility Within Your Organization.

Corporate Social Responsibility (CSR) is a growing priority for businesses of all sizes, as more and more consumers and stakeholders demand that companies operate in an ethical and sustainable manner. In order to build a culture of CSR within your organization, there are several key steps that can be taken.

1. Develop a Clear CSR Vision

The first step in creating a culture of CSR is to develop a clear vision for what you hope to achieve. This vision should be aligned with your company's values and goals, and should be communicated clearly and regularly to all stakeholders. Consider the environmental and social impacts of your operations, and identify areas where your company can make a positive difference.

2. Set Goals and Targets

Once you have developed a clear CSR vision, the next step is to set goals and targets that will help you achieve that vision. These goals should be specific, measurable, achievable, relevant, and time-bound (SMART), and should be developed in consultation with key stakeholders, including employees, customers, and investors. Examples of goals might include reducing your carbon footprint, increasing the diversity of your workforce, or sourcing more sustainable materials for your products.

3. Build a CSR Team

Creating a culture of CSR requires dedicated resources, so it is important to build a team that is focused on these issues. This team should be led by a senior executive who has the authority to make decisions and allocate resources, and should include representatives from different departments within the company. Consider hiring a CSR manager or director to oversee these efforts and ensure that they are integrated into the company's overall strategy.

4. *Engage Employees*

Employees are critical to the success of any CSR initiative, so it is important to engage them early and often in the process. This might involve offering training and development opportunities related to sustainability and social responsibility, or creating employee volunteer programs that allow staff to give back to their communities. Consider also integrating CSR goals and targets into employee performance evaluations, to ensure that everyone in the company is working towards these goals.

5. *Collaborate with External Stakeholders*

In order to build a culture of CSR, it is important to engage with external stakeholders, including customers, suppliers, and local communities. Seek feedback from these stakeholders on your CSR initiatives, and incorporate their ideas and suggestions into your planning and decision-making. Consider also partnering with other organizations that share your values and goals, in order to amplify your impact and achieve your goals more efficiently.

6. *Measure and Report on Progress*

Measuring and reporting on your CSR progress is essential for maintaining accountability and transparency, and for demonstrating the impact of your efforts. Develop key performance indicators (KPIs) that allow you to track progress towards your goals, and report regularly on these KPIs to all stakeholders. Consider also seeking third-party verification of your CSR achievements, to provide independent validation of your efforts.

7. *Continuously Improve*

Finally, creating a culture of CSR requires a commitment to continuous improvement. This means regularly reviewing your goals and targets, seeking feedback from stakeholders, and identifying areas where you can do better. Consider also integrating CSR goals and targets into your overall business strategy, to ensure that sustainability and social responsibility are at the heart of everything you do.

In conclusion, *creating a culture of CSR requires a long-term commitment to sustainability and social responsibility, and requires dedicated resources, clear goals, and ongoing engagement with stakeholders. By following these steps, however, companies can build a strong foundation for ethical and sustainable operations, and can make a positive impact on the world around them.*

e) Measuring and Reporting on Your Sustainability Progress to Stakeholders.

Measuring and reporting on your sustainability progress is a crucial aspect of corporate social responsibility (CSR). It provides stakeholders with transparency and accountability on your sustainability practices, and enables you to track your progress and identify areas for improvement. In this topic we will discuss the key steps involved in measuring and reporting on sustainability progress to stakeholders.

1. Establish a Sustainability Framework

Before you can measure and report on your sustainability progress, it's important to establish a sustainability framework. This involves defining the sustainability goals and targets for your business, and determining the key performance indicators (KPIs) that will be used to track progress. These KPIs should align with your business strategy and values, and should be specific, measurable, and relevant to your sustainability goals.

2. Collect Sustainability Data

Once you have established your sustainability framework, you will need to collect data on your sustainability practices. This involves gathering data on environmental, social, and governance (ESG) factors, such as energy usage, waste production, employee diversity, and community engagement. You can use a variety of methods to collect this data, including surveys, audits, and monitoring systems.

3. Analyze Sustainability Data

After collecting sustainability data, the next step is to analyze the data to identify trends, patterns, and areas for improvement. This involves reviewing the KPIs that were established in the sustainability framework, and comparing them to current performance data. By analyzing the data, you can identify where your business is excelling and where improvements can be made.

4. Report on Sustainability Progress

Once you have collected and analyzed sustainability data, it's time to report on your progress to stakeholders. Reporting on sustainability progress should be transparent, accurate, and timely. You can use a variety of methods to report on your progress, including sustainability reports, annual reports, and integrated reports. It's important to tailor your reporting to the needs of your stakeholders, and to ensure that the information is presented in a clear and understandable way.

5. Use Sustainability Reporting to Drive Continuous Improvement

Sustainability reporting should not be a one-time event. Rather, it should be used as a tool to drive continuous improvement and promote accountability within your business. By analyzing sustainability data and reporting on progress, you can identify areas for improvement and set new sustainability goals and targets. It's important to use sustainability reporting as a way to promote a culture of sustainability within your business, and to encourage all stakeholders to play a role in achieving sustainability goals.

In conclusion, *measuring and reporting on sustainability progress is a critical component of corporate social responsibility. By establishing a sustainability framework, collecting and analyzing sustainability data, reporting on progress, and using reporting to drive continuous improvement, your business can demonstrate its commitment to sustainability and promote transparency and accountability to stakeholders.*

5. SCALING AND GROWING THE BUSINESS

"The best way to predict the future is to create it." - *Peter Drucker*

Scaling and growing a business is a complex and challenging process that requires careful planning and execution. As a visionary entrepreneur, it's important to keep the core vision and values of the business in mind, while also being open to new opportunities and possibilities for growth.

One key strategy for scaling and growing a business is to focus on building a strong team. This means hiring talented individuals who share the company's vision and values, and who have the skills and expertise needed to take the business to the next level. It also means investing in ongoing training and development programs to help employees stay up-to-date with the latest trends and technologies in their respective fields.

Another important strategy for scaling and growing a business is to be open to new ideas and opportunities. This might mean exploring new markets, expanding product lines, or investing in new technologies or processes that can help the business operate more efficiently and effectively.

At the same time, it's important for visionary entrepreneurs to remain focused on the core mission and purpose of the business. This means staying true to the values and principles that guide the company, even as it grows and evolves over time.

By balancing these various factors and approaches, visionary entrepreneurs can successfully scale and grow their businesses, while maintaining a strong sense of purpose and direction.

Visionary entrepreneurs are not content with small-scale success – they want to make a big impact. In this topic, we will explore strategies for scaling and growing a business while maintaining the core vision and values that guide it.

a) Developing a Growth Strategy that Aligns with Your Vision and Values.

Developing a growth strategy that aligns with your vision and values is an essential aspect of building a sustainable and successful business. A growth strategy outlines how a company plans to grow and expand its operations, revenue, and customer base over a specified period. However, growth for growth's sake can lead to unintended consequences, such as sacrificing quality or integrity for short-term gains.

A growth strategy that aligns with your vision and values should consider the following steps:

1. Define your vision and values

Before developing a growth strategy, it's essential to have a clear understanding of your company's vision and values. Your vision should be the guiding star that directs your company's growth strategy, while your values serve as a moral compass that helps ensure you stay true to your principles.

2. Assess your current position

Before creating a growth strategy, it's important to evaluate your current position in the market. Conduct a SWOT analysis to identify your company's strengths, weaknesses, opportunities, and threats. This analysis will help you identify areas where you can capitalize on your strengths and address areas of weakness.

3. Identify your target market

A growth strategy should focus on reaching your ideal customers. Identify your target market and create buyer personas to understand their needs, preferences, and behaviors. This will help you create products and services that align with their needs and provide value to them.

4. Analyze your competition

Analyze your competitors to understand their strengths, weaknesses, and market position. This analysis will help you identify areas of differentiation and competitive advantages that you can leverage in your growth strategy.

5. Develop growth objectives

Based on your vision, values, and market analysis, develop growth objectives that align with your company's mission. These objectives should be specific, measurable, achievable, relevant, and time-bound.

6. Identify growth strategies

Identify growth strategies that align with your growth objectives. These strategies could include expanding your product line, entering new markets, acquiring complementary businesses, or investing in research and development.

7. Prioritize growth initiatives

Once you have identified growth strategies, prioritize them based on their alignment with your vision and values, potential return on investment, and resources required to implement them.

8. Develop an action plan

Develop an action plan for implementing your growth strategies. This plan should outline specific actions, timelines, and responsible parties for each growth initiative.

9. Monitor and adjust

Monitor the progress of your growth initiatives and adjust your strategies as needed. Regularly reviewing your growth objectives and strategies will help ensure that you stay aligned with your vision and values.

In conclusion, *developing a growth strategy that aligns with your vision and values is essential for building a sustainable and successful business. By following these steps, you can create a growth strategy that leverages your strengths, addresses your weaknesses, and provides value to your customers, all while staying true to your principles.*

b) Identifying Key Metrics for Measuring Growth and Success.

Identifying key metrics for measuring growth and success is a crucial step in developing a successful business strategy. These metrics should be aligned with your company's goals and values, and should provide a clear understanding of your business's performance. By tracking and analyzing these metrics, you can identify areas for improvement and make data-driven decisions to drive growth and success.

Here are some key metrics that can help you measure growth and success in your business:

1. Revenue

Revenue is a key indicator of a company's financial performance and growth. Tracking revenue over time can help you understand how your business is performing financially and identify trends in sales and profitability.

2. Customer Acquisition Cost (CAC)

CAC is the cost of acquiring a new customer, including marketing and sales expenses. By tracking CAC over time, you can identify trends in customer acquisition costs and determine whether your marketing and sales efforts are effective.

3. Customer Lifetime Value (CLV)

CLV is the amount of revenue a customer is expected to generate over the course of their relationship with your company. Tracking CLV can help you understand the value of your customer base and identify opportunities to increase revenue through retention and upselling.

4. Conversion Rate

Conversion rate is the percentage of website visitors who take a desired action, such as making a purchase or filling out a lead form. Tracking conversion rates can help you identify areas for improvement in your website or marketing efforts.

5. Net Promoter Score (NPS)

NPS is a measure of customer satisfaction and loyalty. By surveying customers and tracking NPS over time, you can identify areas where your business is excelling and areas where you may need to improve.

6. Employee Engagement:

Employee engagement is a key factor in company culture and can have a significant impact on productivity and retention. By surveying employees and tracking engagement over time, you can identify areas where your company culture is thriving and areas where you may need to make improvements.

7. Social and Environmental Impact

Measuring your company's social and environmental impact can help you demonstrate your commitment to sustainability and corporate social responsibility. Metrics such as carbon footprint, waste reduction, and community engagement can help you understand your impact and identify opportunities for improvement.

By tracking these and other key metrics, you can gain a comprehensive understanding of your business's performance and identify areas for improvement. This data can then be used to develop strategies to drive growth and success while staying true to your company's values and vision.

c) Building a Strong Leadership Team to Support Growth.

Building a strong leadership team is a critical component of supporting growth in any organization. A leadership team plays a pivotal role in shaping the direction and culture of the company, setting goals, and providing guidance to employees. A strong leadership team not only ensures that the organization is operating efficiently and effectively but also creates a supportive and motivating environment for employees.

Here are some key strategies for building a strong leadership team to support growth:

1. Define the Roles and Responsibilities

Before hiring for any leadership position, it is important to define the roles and responsibilities associated with the position. This includes creating a job description that clearly outlines the responsibilities, expectations, and requirements of the position. By defining these parameters upfront, you can better align the skills and experience of potential candidates with the needs of the organization.

2. Hire for the Right Fit

When hiring for leadership positions, it is important to consider not only the candidate's skills and experience but also their values and work style. You want to find candidates who share your organization's vision and values and can work collaboratively with the existing team. The right fit will bring new perspectives and skills while also contributing to a positive company culture.

3. Develop a Succession Plan

A strong leadership team requires planning for the future. By creating a succession plan, you can identify potential candidates for leadership roles and prepare them for future opportunities. This not only helps to ensure a smooth transition when current leaders depart but also provides opportunities for employee growth and development.

4. Provide   Professional   Development Opportunities

Developing the skills and abilities of your leadership team is essential for supporting growth. Providing professional development opportunities, such as workshops, conferences, and mentoring programs, can help leaders to stay up-to-date on the latest industry trends and best practices. Additionally, it shows your commitment to supporting their growth and development, which can contribute to increased employee loyalty and retention.

5. Encourage Collaboration and Communication

A strong leadership team works collaboratively and communicates effectively. Encouraging regular communication and collaboration between leaders can help to ensure that everyone is on the same page and working towards shared goals. This includes regular check-ins, team-building activities, and establishing channels for feedback and input.

6. Foster Accountability

Accountability is essential for ensuring that everyone is working towards shared goals and objectives. Establishing clear expectations, tracking progress, and providing regular feedback can help to ensure that leaders are held accountable for their actions and decisions. Additionally, this can create a culture of continuous improvement, where leaders are motivated to learn and grow.

7. Lead by Example

Finally, building a strong leadership team requires leading by example. As a leader, you set the tone for the organization and influence the behavior of others. By modeling the behavior you expect from others, you can inspire your team to be their best selves and contribute to the growth and success of the organization.

In summary, *building a strong leadership team is essential for supporting growth in any organization. By defining roles and responsibilities, hiring for the right fit, developing a succession plan, providing professional development opportunities, encouraging collaboration and communication, fostering accountability, and leading by example, you can create a team of leaders that supports your organization's vision and values.*

d) Developing Partnerships and Collaborations to Support Expansion.

Developing partnerships and collaborations is an important strategy for businesses looking to support their expansion efforts. By forming strategic partnerships, businesses can access new markets, gain new customers, and take advantage of new opportunities. Collaboration can also help businesses share resources and knowledge, leading to greater innovation and growth.

Here are some key considerations for businesses looking to develop partnerships and collaborations to support expansion:

1. Identify the right partners

When considering potential partners, businesses should look for organizations that share their values and goals. This can include companies in related industries, organizations with complementary products or services, or nonprofits with a similar mission. It's also important to consider factors such as size, reputation, and geographic location when selecting partners.

2. Build relationships

Once potential partners have been identified, businesses should focus on building strong relationships with them. This can involve attending industry events, reaching out to potential partners directly, and engaging with them on social media. By building relationships, businesses can gain a better understanding of their partners' needs and priorities, and identify areas where collaboration could be mutually beneficial.

3. *Define roles and responsibilities*

Once partnerships have been established, it's important to define the roles and responsibilities of each partner. This can involve creating a formal agreement that outlines the goals of the partnership, the resources each partner will contribute, and how the partnership will be managed. Clear communication is key to ensuring that each partner understands their role and is able to contribute effectively.

4. *Create a shared vision*

Successful partnerships are built on a shared vision and goals. To support expansion efforts, businesses should work with their partners to identify shared goals and develop a plan for achieving them. This can involve setting joint targets, creating shared marketing campaigns, or collaborating on new product development.

5. *Foster open communication*

Open communication is essential to the success of any partnership. Businesses should establish regular communication channels with their partners, and ensure that both parties have a clear understanding of each other's goals and priorities. This can involve regular check-ins, joint planning sessions, and ongoing collaboration on shared projects.

6. *Measure success*

To ensure that partnerships are delivering results, businesses should establish clear metrics for success. This can involve tracking the performance of joint projects, measuring the impact of shared marketing campaigns, or monitoring customer feedback. By regularly measuring success, businesses can identify areas where they need to improve and ensure that partnerships are delivering the desired results.

In summary, *developing partnerships and collaborations is* *an important strategy for businesses looking to support their expansion efforts. By identifying the right partners, building strong relationships, defining roles and responsibilities, creating a shared vision, fostering open communication, and measuring success, businesses can successfully collaborate with other organizations to drive growth and innovation.*

e) Identifying and Mitigating Potential Risks Associated with Rapid Growth.

As a business grows and expands, it's natural to experience some level of risk. However, rapid growth can lead to significant challenges that can impact the long-term success of a business. It's important for business leaders to identify potential risks associated with rapid growth and develop strategies to mitigate them

Some of the potential risks associated with rapid growth and strategies for mitigating those risks are as follows :-

1. Overextended Finances

One of the most common risks associated with rapid growth is overextended finances. When a business grows quickly, it can be tempting to invest heavily in new equipment, employees, or marketing efforts. However, if the growth is not sustainable, the business may not be able to generate enough revenue to cover these expenses. This can lead to cash flow problems and potentially even bankruptcy.

To mitigate this risk, it's important for businesses to create realistic growth projections and closely monitor their finances. Business leaders should work closely with their financial teams to ensure that they are not overextending themselves and that they have enough cash on hand to weather any unexpected challenges.

2. Loss of Control

As a business grows, it can become more difficult to maintain control over all aspects of the operation. This can lead to a loss of quality control, customer service issues, and other challenges that can impact the long-term success of the business.

To mitigate this risk, businesses should establish clear policies and procedures for all aspects of their operation. This includes everything from hiring and training employees to quality control and customer service. By creating a strong foundation of policies and procedures, businesses can ensure that they maintain control over all aspects of their operation, even as they continue to grow.

3. Lack of Scalability

Another potential risk associated with rapid growth is a lack of scalability. When a business grows quickly, it can be difficult to scale their operations to meet the increased demand. This can lead to quality control issues, delays in production, and other challenges that can impact the long-term success of the business.

To mitigate this risk, businesses should plan for scalability from the outset. This means investing in infrastructure and systems that can be easily scaled as the business grows. It also means having a plan in place for hiring and training new employees to ensure that the business can meet increased demand without sacrificing quality or customer service.

4. Cultural Challenges

As a business grows, it can become more difficult to maintain a cohesive culture. This can lead to employee turnover, decreased morale, and other challenges that can impact the long-term success of the business.

To mitigate this risk, businesses should prioritize their culture from the outset. This means establishing a clear mission, vision, and set of values that guide all aspects of the operation. It also means creating a strong employee on-boarding and training program that emphasizes the importance of the company culture.

5. Legal and Regulatory Compliance

As a business grows, it can become more complex to comply with legal and regulatory requirements. This can lead to fines, legal challenges, and other challenges that can impact the long-term success of the business.

To mitigate this risk, businesses should work closely with legal and regulatory experts to ensure that they are complying with all applicable laws and regulations. They should also establish clear policies and procedures for compliance and conduct regular audits to ensure that they are staying on track.

In conclusion, *rapid growth can be exciting, but it also comes with significant risks. Business leaders should identify potential risks associated with rapid growth and develop strategies to mitigate them. By doing so, they can ensure that their business continues to thrive even as it continues to expand.*

6. COLLABORATING WITH STAKEHOLDERS

"Collaboration is the key to success for any organization, as it brings together diverse perspectives and skills to achieve a common goal." - Simon Mainwaring

Collaborating with stakeholders is a crucial aspect of building a successful business. Whether it's working with suppliers, customers, employees, or investors, entrepreneurs must establish strong relationships and partnerships to achieve their goals. This topic explores the importance of collaborating with stakeholders and how it can lead to long-term success.

As the business landscape becomes more complex and interconnected, collaboration has become a key driver of innovation and growth. By working with stakeholders, entrepreneurs can tap into new ideas, expertise, and resources, enabling them to solve complex challenges and seize new opportunities. Collaboration also helps to build trust and loyalty among stakeholders, creating a strong foundation for long-term success.

Effective collaboration requires strong communication, trust, and mutual respect. Entrepreneurs must be able to listen to their stakeholders, understand their needs and perspectives, and work together to achieve common goals. They must also be willing to take risks and experiment with new approaches, recognizing that collaboration is not always easy or straightforward.

Building a future through purposeful innovation requires collaboration with a variety of stakeholders, including employees, customers, investors, and community members. In this topic , we will explore how to build strong relationships with stakeholders, and how to align their interests with those of the business.

a) Building Strong Relationships with Customers and Clients.

Building strong relationships with customers and clients is critical for the success and growth of any business. A strong relationship with customers leads to brand loyalty, increased sales, positive word-of-mouth marketing, and a better understanding of their needs and expectations

Let's discuss the key steps in building strong relationships with customers and clients.

1. Understand Your Customers

The first step in building strong relationships with customers is to understand their needs, preferences, and expectations. Conducting market research and gathering customer feedback can help you gain insights into what your customers want and need from your products or services. This information can be used to tailor your offerings to better meet their needs, as well as to improve customer service and support.

2. Provide Excellent Customer Service

Providing excellent customer service is essential to building strong relationships with customers. This means being responsive to their needs, resolving issues quickly and effectively, and going above and beyond to exceed their expectations. Providing a positive customer experience at every touchpoint can help build trust and loyalty, and can lead to positive word-of-mouth recommendations.

3. Build Trust and Credibility

Building trust and credibility with your customers is another important aspect of building strong relationships. This can be achieved by being transparent and honest in your business dealings, delivering on your promises, and providing high-quality products and services. Trust and credibility are essential for building long-term relationships with customers and can help differentiate your business from competitors.

4. Personalize Your Communications

Personalizing your communications with customers can help build stronger relationships. This can include addressing customers by name, sending personalized emails, and tailoring your marketing messages to their specific interests and needs. By showing that you understand and care about your customers on an individual level, you can build a stronger emotional connection with them.

5. Engage with Customers on Social Media

Social media provides an opportunity to engage with customers in a more informal and personal way. By responding to customer comments and messages on social media, you can show that you are listening and value their feedback. Sharing content that is relevant and interesting to your customers can also help build engagement and strengthen relationships.

6. Offer Incentives and Rewards

Offering incentives and rewards to customers can help build loyalty and strengthen relationships. This can include discounts, freebies, and loyalty programs that reward customers for repeat purchases. By showing your customers that you appreciate their business and are willing to reward their loyalty, you can build stronger relationships and encourage repeat business.

7. Continuously Improve Your Offerings

Continuously improving your products and services is essential to building strong relationships with customers. This means listening to their feedback, identifying areas for improvement, and making changes to better meet their needs and expectations. By showing that you are committed to delivering the best possible experience for your customers, you can build trust and loyalty and strengthen your relationships over time.

In conclusion, *building strong relationships with customers and clients is critical for the success and growth of any business. By understanding their needs, providing excellent customer service, building trust and credibility, personalizing communications, engaging with customers on social media, offering incentives and rewards, and continuously improving your offerings, you can build stronger relationships and encourage long-term loyalty.*

b) Engaging with The Local Community to Build Trust and Support.

E ngaging with the local community is an essential aspect of building a successful and sustainable business. By establishing strong relationships with the community, businesses can build trust, enhance their reputation, and gain valuable insights into local needs and trends. This can help businesses to tailor their products and services to meet the specific needs of the community, leading to increased customer loyalty and revenue.

Here are some key steps businesses can take to engage with the local community:

1. Participate in local events and initiatives

One of the easiest ways to connect with the community is to participate in local events and initiatives. This can include sponsoring community events such as festivals, fairs, and sports teams, or participating in local charitable causes and volunteer programs.

2. Listen to the community

To effectively engage with the local community, businesses need to understand their needs and concerns. This can be achieved through conducting surveys, focus groups, and other forms of market research to gather feedback and insights from the community. This information can then be used to inform product development and other business decisions

3. Build relationships with local stakeholders

It's important for businesses to build relationships with key stakeholders in the community, such as local government officials, business associations, and community organizations. These stakeholders can provide valuable support and resources, and can help businesses navigate local regulations and policies.

4. Support local economic development

Businesses can support the local economy by sourcing goods and services locally, hiring local workers, and partnering with local suppliers and vendors. This can help to create jobs and stimulate economic growth, while also strengthening the business's relationship with the community.

5. Communicate transparently and honestly

To build trust with the community, businesses need to communicate transparently and honestly. This includes being open and transparent about business practices and operations, and addressing any concerns or complaints in a timely and respectful manner.

6. Be a good neighbor

Businesses can build goodwill in the community by being a good neighbor. This includes being mindful of noise and other disturbances, maintaining clean and well-maintained facilities, and taking steps to minimize any negative environmental impacts.

By taking these steps, businesses can build strong relationships with the local community, which can help to support their growth and success over the long term.

c) Developing Partnerships with Other Businesses and Organizations.

Developing partnerships with other businesses and organizations can be a strategic way for companies to expand their reach and impact. By collaborating with other entities, businesses can tap into new markets, pool resources, and leverage expertise to achieve shared goals.

Here are some key benefits of developing partnerships:

1. Access to new markets and customers

By partnering with other businesses or organizations, you can tap into new markets and reach customers you may not have been able to on your own.

2. Shared resources and cost savings

Partnerships can allow companies to share resources and costs, which can be particularly beneficial for small businesses with limited resources.

3. Leveraging expertise

Partnering with other organizations can provide access to specialized expertise that your company may not have in-house. This can help you to develop new products or services, or improve existing ones.

4. Increased innovation:

Collaboration with other entities can help foster innovation by bringing together diverse perspectives and ideas.

5. Improved reputation

Partnering with respected and well-regarded organizations can improve your own company's reputation and legitimacy.

Here Are Some Key Steps In Developing Successful Partnerships:

1. **Identify potential partners:** Identify businesses or organizations that share similar values and goals, and that can complement or supplement your own offerings.

2. **Build relationships:** Once you have identified potential partners, invest in building relationships with them. Attend networking events, conferences, and other industry gatherings to meet potential partners and learn about their goals and needs.

3. **Develop a shared vision:** Work with your partners to develop a shared vision and strategy for your partnership. Be clear about what each partner brings to the table, and how you will work together to achieve your goals.

4. **Establish clear roles and responsibilities:** Once you have developed a shared vision, establish clear roles and responsibilities for each partner. Be sure to define how decisions will be made, and how resources will be shared.

5. **Monitor progress:** Regularly monitor your progress and assess the success of your partnership. Be willing to adjust your strategy and make changes as necessary to ensure that you are meeting your shared goals.

6. ***Communicate effectively:*** Effective communication is critical to successful partnerships. Be sure to keep all partners informed about progress and any changes to the partnership.

7. ***Nurture the relationship:*** It's important to continually nurture your partnerships and invest in building and maintaining strong relationships. This can involve regular meetings, joint projects, and other activities that reinforce your shared goals and vision.

Conclusion

In conclusion, building a successful and sustainable business requires a combination of factors, including a clear vision and values, effective leadership, innovation, and a commitment to social responsibility and sustainability. By focusing on these key areas, businesses can create a strong foundation for growth and success, while also making a positive impact on their employees, customers, and the world around them.

It's important to remember that building a successful business takes time, effort, and ongoing commitment. However, by staying focused on your goals and values, and by working collaboratively with key stakeholders, you can create a business that not only thrives financially, but also makes a positive impact on the world.

d) Working Closely with Investors to Align Interests and Drive Growth.

Working closely with investors is a crucial aspect of building a successful and sustainable business. Investors provide financial support, strategic guidance, and often bring valuable industry expertise to the table. However, to ensure that investors and the business are aligned in their interests, it's important to establish a strong working relationship and to communicate openly and transparently.

Here are some key steps to working closely with investors to align interests and drive growth:

1. ***Identify and attract the right investors***: It's important to seek out investors who share your vision and values, and who are aligned with your business goals. This involves conducting thorough research to identify potential investors who have experience and expertise in your industry, and who have a track record of supporting sustainable and socially responsible businesses.

2. ***Establish clear communication channels:*** Effective communication is essential for building a strong relationship with investors. This involves setting up regular meetings to discuss progress and challenges, sharing regular updates on business operations and financial performance, and being transparent about any potential risks or obstacles.

3. ***Develop a shared vision for growth:*** It's important

to work collaboratively with investors to develop a shared vision for the future of the business. This involves identifying key growth opportunities, setting realistic goals and targets, and developing a clear roadmap for achieving these objectives.\

4. ***Align incentives and compensation structures:*** To ensure that investors are motivated to support long-term growth and success, it's important to align incentives and compensation structures with the business's goals and values. This involves developing a compensation structure that rewards long-term success, rather than short-term gains.

5. ***Monitor and report on progress:*** To build trust and confidence with investors, it's important to monitor and report on progress regularly. This involves developing key performance indicators (KPIs) to track progress against goals, and providing regular updates on financial performance and operational metrics.

6. ***Continuously communicate and seek feedback:*** To ensure that the business and investors remain aligned in their interests, it's important to continuously communicate and seek feedback from investors. This involves regularly soliciting feedback on business operations and strategy, and being open to suggestions for improvement.

By working closely with investors and aligning interests, businesses can build a strong foundation for sustainable growth and success. Through effective communication, shared vision, and a commitment to long-term success, businesses and investors can work together to create value for all stakeholders.

e) Maintaining Open Lines of Communication with All Stakeholders to Ensure Their Needs are Being Met.

Maintaining open lines of communication with all stakeholders is crucial for any business that wants to ensure the needs and expectations of all parties involved are being met. This includes not only investors and customers but also employees, suppliers, regulators, and the wider community.

Effective communication can help build trust and foster positive relationships, leading to greater loyalty and support for the business. It also helps identify potential issues and opportunities early on, allowing for prompt action and minimizing the risk of misunderstandings or conflicts.

Here are some key strategies for maintaining open lines of communication with different stakeholders:

1. Investors:

Regularly report on financial performance and growth prospects, including any risks or challenges that may impact the business. Provide opportunities for investors to ask questions and provide feedback, and be transparent about any decisions that may affect their interests.

2. Customers:

Listen to feedback and complaints, and respond promptly and professionally. Use social media and other channels to engage with customers and build relationships, and provide opportunities for them to provide input on new products or services.

3. Employees:

Encourage open and honest communication among team members, and provide regular feedback and coaching to help them grow and develop. Provide opportunities for employees to provide input on company policies and practices, and be transparent about any decisions that may impact their roles or job security.

4. Suppliers:

Build relationships based on trust and mutual benefit, and communicate regularly on any changes or challenges that may impact the supply chain. Provide opportunities for suppliers to provide input on product design or production processes, and be transparent about any issues or delays that may impact their delivery schedules.

5. Regulators

Maintain open lines of communication with regulators, and ensure compliance with all relevant laws and regulations. Provide timely and accurate information on any changes to the business or industry that may impact regulatory requirements, and address any concerns or questions raised by regulators promptly and professionally.

6. Community

Engage with the local community through events, sponsorships, and charitable activities, and listen to their concerns and feedback. Be transparent about any plans or decisions that may impact the local environment or community, and work collaboratively to find solutions that benefit all parties.

Overall, *maintaining open lines of communication requires ongoing effort and commitment from all parties involved. It requires a culture of transparency, trust, and mutual respect, and a willingness to listen and respond to feedback and concerns. However, the benefits* *of effective communication can be significant, including improved relationships, greater loyalty and support, and a more sustainable and successful business.*

7. OVERCOMING CHALLENGES AND SETBACKS

"The greatest glory in living lies not in never falling, but in rising every time we fall." - Nelson Mandela.

L ife is full of challenges and setbacks, and the same holds true for entrepreneurship. In the face of unexpected obstacles, visionary entrepreneurs must learn to adapt and persevere if they want to succeed. This topic will explore strategies for overcoming challenges and setbacks in business, including tips for developing resilience and grit.

Entrepreneurship is a journey that is filled with ups and downs, and it is inevitable that setbacks will occur. From market shifts to unexpected competition, there are numerous obstacles that entrepreneurs may face along the way. However, what separates successful entrepreneurs from those who give up is their ability to overcome these challenges and keep moving forward.

Overcoming challenges and setbacks requires more than just positive thinking – it requires a willingness to learn from failures, to adapt to changing circumstances, and to remain focused on the ultimate vision. By developing resilience and grit, entrepreneurs can bounce back from setbacks stronger than before, and use these experiences to fuel growth and innovation.

In this topic, we will explore strategies for overcoming common challenges in entrepreneurship, such as raising capital, managing cash flow, and dealing with failure. We will also delve into the importance of mindset and attitude in overcoming obstacles, and offer practical tips for developing resilience and perseverance in the face of adversity.

a) Identifying Potential Risks and Challenges Before They Arise.

Identifying potential risks and challenges before they arise is an important aspect of running a successful business. By anticipating and preparing for potential problems, you can mitigate their impact and reduce the likelihood of serious consequences.

Here are some key steps you can take to identify potential risks and challenges before they arise:

1. ***Conduct a risk assessment:*** A risk assessment involves identifying potential risks to your business and evaluating their likelihood and potential impact. This can involve looking at things like market trends, regulatory changes, natural disasters, and cyber security threats.

2. ***Stay up-to-date with industry trends and news***: By staying informed about what's happening in your industry, you can identify potential risks and challenges early on. This can involve subscribing to industry publications, attending conferences and events, and following thought leaders and influencers on social media.

3. ***Regularly review your business operations:*** Conduct regular audits of your business operations to identify areas where risks may be present. This can involve reviewing your financial statements, supply chain processes, and customer data privacy practices.

4. **Encourage open communication with employees:** Your employees are often the first line of defense when it comes to identifying potential risks and challenges. Encourage them to speak up if they notice anything unusual or concerning, and provide a mechanism for reporting potential problems anonymously if necessary.

5. **Develop a crisis management plan:** Even with the best preparation, things can go wrong. Develop a crisis management plan that outlines how your business will respond to different types of crises, and be sure to regularly review and update it.

By taking these steps, you can identify potential risks and challenges before they arise, and develop a plan to mitigate their impact if they do occur. This can help ensure the long-term success and sustainability of your business.

b) Developing Contingency Plans to Mitigate Potential Risks

Developing contingency plans is an essential part of risk management, especially when it comes to running a business. Contingency plans are essentially backup plans that help businesses address unexpected events or situations that could negatively impact their operations. These plans outline a set of actions that can be taken in the event of an emergency or crisis to minimize disruptions and maintain continuity.

- Developing a contingency plan involves a number of key steps. The first step is to identify the potential risks that could impact your business. These risks could be related to a wide range of factors, including natural disasters, cyber attacks, financial downturns, supply chain disruptions, or sudden changes in market demand.

- Once you have identified the potential risks, the next step is to assess their likelihood and impact. This involves evaluating the probability of the risk occurring, as well as the potential impact it could have on your business operations. This information can then be used to prioritize the risks and determine which ones are the most critical to address.

- After prioritizing the risks, the next step is to develop a set of contingency plans that can be implemented in the event of an emergency or crisis. These plans should be designed to address each of the identified risks and should include a clear set of actions that can be taken to minimize the impact of the risk on your business.

- For example, if the risk is related to a supply chain disruption, your contingency plan may include identifying alternative suppliers or developing a plan to shift production to other locations. If the risk is related to a financial downturn, your contingency plan may include cutting expenses, diversifying your product offerings, or seeking out additional sources of funding.

- It is important to remember that contingency plans are not one-size-fits-all. The best plans are tailored to the specific needs and circumstances of your business. They should also be regularly reviewed and updated as new risks emerge or as your business operations change.

- In addition to developing contingency plans, it is also important to communicate these plans to key stakeholders, including employees, customers, suppliers, and investors. This can help to build trust and confidence in your business and ensure that everyone is on the same page in the event of an emergency or crisis.

- Overall, developing contingency plans is an essential part of risk management for any business. By identifying potential risks, assessing their likelihood and impact, and developing clear plans to address them, businesses can better prepare themselves for unexpected events and minimize the impact of these events on their operations.

c) Learning from Failures and Setbacks to Improve Future Decision-Making.

Learning from failures and setbacks is a critical part of achieving long-term success in any business. It allows entrepreneurs to identify what went wrong and develop new strategies to avoid similar mistakes in the future. This process of continuous improvement is essential for growth and can help organizations achieve their goals more efficiently.

Here are some key ways that entrepreneurs can learn from failures and setbacks:

1. Analyze what went wrong:

The first step in learning from a failure or setback is to analyze what happened. Entrepreneurs should take the time to examine the situation in detail, looking at all the factors that contributed to the failure. This could involve gathering data, interviewing team members, or seeking outside perspectives from industry experts. The goal is to gain a comprehensive understanding of what went wrong and why.

2. Identify patterns:

Once the analysis is complete, it's important to look for patterns or commonalities across different failures or setbacks. For example, if multiple projects have failed due to poor communication, it may be necessary to invest in better communication tools or training for team members. Identifying these patterns can help entrepreneurs make strategic decisions about where to focus their efforts in the future.

3. Take responsibility:

It's important for entrepreneurs to take responsibility for failures and setbacks. This means acknowledging mistakes and taking steps to address them. Blaming others or external factors may be tempting, but it's not productive. Instead, entrepreneurs should focus on what they can control and work to improve their processes and systems.

4. Develop a plan:

Once entrepreneurs have analyzed the situation and identified patterns, it's time to develop a plan for moving forward. This could involve making changes to processes, systems, or team structure. The plan should be specific, measurable, and time-bound, with clear milestones and metrics for success.

5. Communicate the plan:

Communicating the plan to stakeholders is critical for success. This could include team members, investors, or customers. By being transparent about the plan and the steps being taken to address the failure or setback, entrepreneurs can build trust and credibility with stakeholders.

6. Monitor progress:

Once the plan is in place, it's important to monitor progress and adjust as necessary. Regular check-ins can help entrepreneurs stay on track and identify new challenges as they arise. It's also important to celebrate successes along the way, no matter how small.

7. Learn from successes:

Learning from successes is just as important as learning from failures. Entrepreneurs should take the time to analyze what went right and why. This can help them replicate success in the future and build on their strengths as an organization.

In conclusion, *learning from failures and setbacks is an essential part of achieving long-term success in any business. It requires entrepreneurs to analyze what went wrong, identify patterns,* *take responsibility, develop a plan, communicate the plan, monitor progress, and learn from successes. By embracing failure as an opportunity for growth, entrepreneurs can build more resilient and successful organizations.*

d) Building Resilience and Adaptability in the Face of Uncertainty.

Building resilience and adaptability are critical for any business to succeed in the face of uncertainty. The global economy has always been unpredictable, but the events of the past year have demonstrated the importance of being prepared for unexpected challenges.

In This Topic, We'll Explore Strategies For Building Resilience And Adaptability Into Your Business, So You Can Weather The Storms And Come Out Stronger On The Other Side.

1. Embrace a Growth Mindset

The first step to building resilience and adaptability is to embrace a growth mindset. This means adopting a perspective that sees challenges as opportunities for growth and improvement, rather than setbacks. Leaders who cultivate a growth mindset are more likely to be flexible and adaptable in the face of uncertainty, as they are focused on learning and growing from every experience.

2. Prioritize Agility

Agility is another key factor in building resilience and adaptability. The ability to pivot quickly in response to changing circumstances is critical for businesses that want to survive and thrive in a rapidly changing environment. To be agile, businesses need to be able to identify opportunities and risks quickly and adjust their strategies accordingly.

3. Diversify Your Business

Diversification is an important strategy for building resilience and adaptability. By expanding your offerings, you can weather downturns in one area of your business by relying on other areas that are performing well. Diversification can also help you identify new opportunities for growth and innovation.

4. Build Strong Relationships

Building strong relationships with customers, suppliers, and other stakeholders is crucial for building resilience and adaptability. When you have strong relationships, you can rely on others for support during difficult times. Additionally, by engaging with customers and suppliers, you can better understand their needs and adjust your business strategies accordingly.

5. Focus on Innovation

Innovation is another key factor in building resilience and adaptability. By constantly seeking out new ideas and approaches, businesses can stay ahead of the curve and remain competitive in the face of uncertainty. Focusing on innovation can also help businesses identify new revenue streams and opportunities for growth.

6. Build a Strong Team

Building a strong team is critical for building resilience and adaptability. When you have a team of talented and motivated individuals, you can respond quickly to changing circumstances and identify new opportunities for growth. Additionally, by investing in employee development and training, you can build a culture of continuous learning and improvement.

7. Develop Contingency Plans

Finally, businesses that want to build resilience and adaptability need to have contingency plans in place. These plans should outline the steps your business will take in response to different scenarios, such as an economic downturn, a natural disaster, or a public health crisis. By having contingency plans in place, you can respond quickly and effectively to unexpected challenges, and minimize the impact on your business.

In conclusion, building resilience and adaptability is critical for businesses that want to succeed in an uncertain world. By embracing a growth mindset, prioritizing agility, diversifying your business, building strong relationships, focusing on innovation, building a strong team, and developing contingency plans, you can position your business to thrive in the face of uncertainty.

e) Staying Focused on the Long-Term Vision and Mission, Even When Facing Short-Term Challenges.

S taying focused on the long-term vision and mission, even when facing short-term challenges, is a crucial aspect of building a successful business. Short-term challenges and setbacks are inevitable in any business, but it's important to maintain a clear sense of direction and purpose in order to stay motivated and keep moving forward.

One way to stay focused on the long-term vision is to regularly revisit and update the company's mission and vision statements. These statements should serve as guiding principles for all decision-making and should be revisited periodically to ensure they are still relevant and aligned with the company's goals.

Another way to maintain focus on the long-term vision is to establish a set of core values that guide the company's culture and behavior. These values should be reflected in everything from hiring and employee training to marketing and customer interactions.

It's also important to foster a sense of resilience and adaptability within the organization. This can be done by encouraging employees to take risks and try new approaches, while also providing support and resources to help them overcome any obstacles they may encounter.

Finally, it's important to maintain a positive and optimistic outlook, even when facing challenging circumstances. This can be achieved through regular team-building exercises, open communication, and a willingness to learn from mistakes and failures. By staying focused on the long-term vision and mission, building resilience and adaptability, and maintaining a positive outlook, businesses can overcome short-term challenges and achieve long-term success.

In conclusion, the success of a business is determined by various factors, including the identification and prioritization of key stakeholders, creating a strong vision and values statement, encouraging creativity and collaboration among employees, investing in emerging technologies, implementing sustainable practices, building strong partnerships and collaborations, maintaining open communication with all stakeholders, and developing a culture of corporate social responsibility.

To achieve these goals, businesses must develop effective strategies and contingency plans, maintain a growth mindset, learn from failures, and build resilience and adaptability. Additionally, working closely with investors, focusing on long-term goals, and prioritizing the needs of all stakeholders are essential for sustainable growth and success.

By prioritizing these key areas, businesses can build a strong foundation for success, aligning their operations with their core values and mission, and driving growth and innovation for the long term.

In conclusion, visionary entrepreneurship is about building a future through purposeful innovation. It is about identifying opportunities, solving problems, and creating value in a way that benefits society as a whole. To be a visionary entrepreneur, it is important to have a clear vision, a strong sense of purpose, and a willingness to take risks. By embracing innovation, being open to new ideas, and continually learning and adapting, visionary entrepreneurs can create businesses that have a lasting impact on the world.

Through the strategies and insights shared in this book,

entrepreneurs can gain a better understanding of what it takes to build a successful and sustainable business. By developing a clear vision, prioritizing innovation, focusing on customer needs, building a strong team, embracing technology, and pursuing purpose-driven goals, entrepreneurs can build businesses that not only generate profits but also have a positive impact on the world.

As we look to the future, it is clear that visionary entrepreneurship will continue to play a critical role in shaping the world we live in. By embracing purposeful innovation and building businesses that prioritize sustainability, entrepreneurs can help to create a better future for all.

POINTS TO PONDER
ON EACH 7 KEYS.

1. Developing A Vision And Mission

•   What values are most important to your organization, and how do they inform your vision and mission?
•   How do you ensure that your vision and mission are aligned with the needs and wants of your target audience?
•   How do you measure progress towards your vision and mission, and how often do you review and adjust them?

2. Innovation

•   How do you encourage creativity and idea generation within your organization?
•   How do you provide resources and support for experimentation with new technologies and ideas?
•   How do you measure the impact of innovation on your organization, and use that information to inform future decisions?

3. Investing In Technology

•   What types of technology would be most beneficial for your organization, and how do you prioritize investments?
•   How do you ensure that investments in technology align with your business goals and values?
•   How do you measure the impact of technology investments

on your organization, and how do you make decisions about future investments?

4. Sustainable Growth

•   How do you balance short-term growth with long-term sustainability?
•   What key metrics do you use to measure growth and success, and how do you ensure that they align with your vision and values?
•   How do you mitigate risks associated with rapid growth and maintain strong relationships with stakeholders?

5. Corporate Social Responsibility

•   How do you identify areas of environmental and social impact within your organization?
•   How do you set targets for reducing your carbon footprint and other environmental impacts?
•   How do you foster a culture of corporate social responsibility within your organization, and measure progress towards your goals?

6. Collaboration And Teamwork

•   How do you foster a collaborative culture within your organization?
•   What strategies do you use to promote teamwork and communication?
•   How do you measure the impact of collaboration and teamwork on your organization and make adjustments as needed?

7. Risk Management And Adaptability

•   How do you identify potential risks and challenges before they arise?
•   How do you develop contingency plans to mitigate risks?
•   How do you build resilience and adaptability in the face of

uncertainty, and learn from failures and setbacks?

ABOUT THE AUTHOR

Vishal Vinda Vijay Palyekar

 Vishal Palyekar is an accomplished sales and cold calling expert with a passion for communication and a track record of success in managing brands and products. With strong organizational skills and a positive attitude, Vishal Palyekar is dedicated to working smart and delivering innovative strategies to shape the future of business. Besides consulting work, Vishal is also an avid actor, reader, photographer and athlete who loves inspiring others with his enthusiasm. He has worked on various films, short films, documentaries and television shows as an actor, asst. director, casting director,etc. and also directed & coached theatre productions. Vishal Palyekar holds a Diploma in Acting from The Barry John Acting Studio, Mumbai , Adv. Dip. in Filmmaking & Acting from Shri. Mahesh Rane's Filmcraft Academy, Goa and currently pursuing Bachelors of Social Work from IGNOU.